IMPATIENTLY

Waiting

---Don't Rush Love---

SHEMEKA MCNAIR

Copyright

Impatiently Waiting

Copyright © by Shemeka McNair

For More Information.

Shemeka McNair
PO Box 2228
Orlando, FL 32802

ISBN-13: 978-1-7339718-1-2

Dedication

I dedicate this book to all of those who have been waiting with me. It is Well Worth the Wait.

Table of Contents

Poetry

Acknowledgements

I would like to give all honor and glory to the one who made this happen, God Almighty. I would like to take the time to thank everyone who has supported me through the process My Parents and my Step Parents who have been there for me from a young girl trying to figure it out until now. You have encouraged, pushed and supported me through it all. To my entire Family you ALL have been my strength and my inspiration, you always showed up and been there for me. Thank you all for believing in me from day one. My Sisters and Cousins Group messages are too live that is all I can say, thank you all for that outlet. To my friends Oh God, it has been a rough ride you all know the stuff I couldn't tell anybody.

Each of you I have shared information that I didn't with the other that is my way of making you Individually Special to me. Thank you so much for listening. Thanks for answering my calls at 2:00 a.m. 3:00 a.m. and 4:00 a.m. helping me to piece my heart back together. To my Leader, other Leaders and everyone in their respective places I appreciate the PRAYERS, thank you for the mentorship, the relationship class, the prophecies, interpretations of my dreams, revelations, and words of encouragement. Thank you for being there.

To all of those who have helped and supported the It's Well Worth the Wait stage play production. I appreciate you and will never forget the role you played in helping my dream come true. To all those that follow me, support me and encourage me on social media thank you. My 102nd Military friends, Magee High school classmates, and teachers, My New York Film Academy classmates thank you.

Thank you for my photographer Lee Hodge for the Banging Cover Picture, a big shout out to Courtney Patterson for the body you see in my cover picture, that was from her being my fitness trainer at the time. Thanks, Christina and Pavis for the Hair and Makeup, Slayage. Shekenyah Harris thank you for being obedient without your write your book boot camp I probably wouldn't have had the courage to publish the book alone. Thank all of you who attempted to help in the process of getting the book release thank you, I'm still going to need you, just hold on. Lol. I would like to give the Biggest Thank You to every guy that purposely took the time out to Break my Heart you made this Possible. You brought me to it, but God took me through it. My girl April added her two cents in on that, but it is true. God Bless You!

Preface

Waiting is not always Easy. Even though we are Impatient at times, God knows our true desire is to wait for what we know is right for us. If you are single and waiting, this book is definitely for you but also, if you're MARRIED OR DIVORCED or just plain out confused about what is going on. This book will help you no matter your current relationship status. After reading this book, you will know how to come out of and avoid Toxic Relationships. This book will prepare you to make better decisions in the mates you choose. Some of the things I have written in this book may not be for you, buy I am sure it will touch someone's life. The process of finding the Love of your Life, Your Helpmeet, or Your Life Partner is not always a walk in the park. You will receive helpful pointers on how to handle the dating process; the forgiving process, the healing process, and the process of moving forward. Be Encouraged: the Love of Your Life is just a Decision Away! Ladies, I know the process is extremely hard, but remain encouraged. I know so well, the pain of trying to figure out who your spouse is; you ask yourself, Lord did I miss him? If I can just help in that area, for now, I will. I have been hurt a million times over, and refuse to let my pain go to waste. I hope some of the things that I have written, will help some women make the decisions they need to walk away from wrong, toxic, and painful relationships.

When you live your life without any form of self-control, it is easy to be single because you can sleep around with your man, someone else's man, etc. But when you are trying to do things the right way, by remaining Holy, waiting on God, the Wait is not easy. It's hard trying to figure out when it will happen. There were so many days I spent talking my friends' ears off, trying to get answers from them, I wanted their opinion, I wanted to know their thoughts, I was desperately trying to figure out this part of my life. There were many nights of me crying on my pillow, crying in my car because this was a process of long-suffering that I did not feel I could take much longer. It is a painful Experience, but I know the results will be so satisfying. This book was birthed out of my pain. I had tears in my eyes as I typed this book. God was saying to me, write about it, tell them what you have learned, I know it hurts but what did that situation teach you, what could you have done differently.

A guy once asked me what qualified me to speak on relationships, or qualified me to tell other people how to wait on the right one when I do not have a man. Well, what qualifies me, is my experience. How can I tell people how to get a good man and I don't have one? Easy; they have a man but who says they have the Right one. My singleness doesn't disqualify me rather; it's Proof that I'm not in a bad relationship! I am not in a bad marriage, and will not enter one. So, in essence, I'm a Successful Single Woman: meaning, I'm successful in being Single and Waiting. I'm experienced in coming out of the wrong Relationship. I'm experienced in leaving abusive Relationships. I'm experienced in Growing and becoming Stronger in my singleness. My past mistakes are my qualifications. Getting a man is nothing. Anyone today can have one, but is that God's man for you? Does he love you the way God commanded him to? So, from whom would you rather hear, the person who is miserable with a man or the Person who is triumphal without one? There is not an extreme shortage of men. There's an extreme shortage of men who will "do right." This isn't true for everybody, but for some, it could feel that way. You have to show a man how to treat you; what you will accept, and what you won't accept.

Testimony

I came from a past of Rejection, Abuse, Depression, Suicide attempts, and Perverted Relationships, as a young girl. All of which, left me with a huge wound in my heart. I didn't trust. I didn't want to love anymore, and to be honest; I never knew how to love properly. Love was strange to me; something I could never quite figure out. Anything that came close to making me feel good inside I thought it was love.

I used to hear the phrase, "Love is Pain." There is some truth in that saying, but where I don't agree, is when the pain is beginning to manifest in physical, emotional, or mental abuse. That is not Love. It is true that love suffereth long and is patient and kind. (See, 1 Corinthians 13:4) That is speaking about a person dying to oneself and not by someone else. Did you catch that? Love doesn't mean it is okay for someone to hurt you, but it is referring to God's love, which causes growth; and something or someone who is slowly killing you inside. I did not have any respect for myself as a woman. I found myself in abusive relationships and even a marriage; one in which the abuse started long before the union occurred. I lost some family and friends because I chose to stay in the relationship. I still married into it. Your marriage or relationship should never pull you away from those whom you love and from those who love you unless it is for the better.

Usually, Men who are controlling and manipulative will try to first, pull you away from those who care and who will reveal the truth to you. They may make you feel that others like your family and friends are not really for you, or care for your best interests. It is all a mind control thing. Never fall for it. Never allow it.

I allowed this man to strip me of every piece of confidence I had. Keywords, "I Allowed." I hated the way I looked. I felt inadequate. I was questioning myself, my worth. I contemplated suicide on several occasions, and I even tried to kill myself over this man. I recall a time in particular, during this relationship, when I overdosed because he broke up with me. (Something he would do on and off.) I would move on, and he would come and break up whatever new relationship I had going on. There were times when I would be afraid to go home to my Mom's or be afraid to be home when my mom would go to work, because he would be hiding outside somewhere to catch me coming, and would jump on me.

He would intentionally try to get me pregnant, and when he thought I was pregnant, he would punch me, repeatedly in my stomach. I would Sob and Cry for him to stop and his response was that he didn't "want a Baby from a Hoe." There was constant fighting; and yes, eventually I was fighting back. If he came to my Mom's house to jump on me and leave, I would drive over to his parents, and try to retaliate. They thought that I was just showing up to their house to cause drama or to bother their son, but that wasn't the case. All of this went on while I was still a child myself, a teenager trying to figure it all out. In the midst of all of that, I still married him. I went away and joined the military.

I became pregnant. I thought that then the abuse would stop, but instead, it became worse. I was being Slapped, Punched, Stomped, and Body Slammed to the Ground while I was pregnant. I stopped fighting back and just took it because I didn't want to lose my child. Imagine, walking around 7-8 months pregnant, with a black eye. I made up stories: "Oh I was trying to break up a fight, and someone elbowed me in the eye." I sounded as silly as I looked. Things never became better I know you think things will eventually get better but will it? I came close to death many times. Ask yourself is it Worth it? Is he Worth it? Why are you willing to take that type of risk? Why take chances with your life? There is a chance you can make it out, and there is a chance that you won't. I will share more of my story in a different book. Let's stay on Topic.

You would think I would have learned my lesson, right? Time passed. I was divorced, and serving God. After seven years of Celibacy Yes; NO Sex, (Here I am, this Strong, Powerful Anointed Woman of God) I finally met someone, but He and I are living two different lifestyles. We vibed together, though. We would chill, every once in a while. He claimed that he understood where I was in my walk with Christ. We discussed how I was waiting for Marriage. If he pressured me for sex, I pressed for "The Ring," so there became a season during which I was going "through" in my spiritual walk.

I had gone through a period of complete warfare, many attacks on my life, I was accused of having sex with people in the church. People were dreaming, scheming, and spreading slander about me. Therefore, I had to attend meetings with individuals who would claim they had a "dream" that I was fornicating, having sex outside of marriage. Then I would be rebuked and shamed because of dreams, lies, and rumors, while in reality, I was truly celibate. Becoming celibate was a decision I made when I first walked away from the altar after rededicating my life to Christ. I decided that I wanted to give myself God wholly. I even broke off my engagement, just to do things completely right.

While going through all of the church drama, life was hitting me. Late one night, I got a text from him around 2:00 a.m. asking me to come over. God always make a way of escape, if we want to take it. I was ignoring God. I was going to press pass conviction and make this happen. Even though my pain wanted to get the best of me, my Spirit was still fighting for me. It is not always fleshly desires that cause us to walk in sin. Sometimes it is undealt with issues, like the pain I was experiencing at the time. It was not sex I wanted. I wanted my Pain to Stop.

After arriving at his place I could not get into the building, so I waited for him to come down, and let me into the garage. 30 minutes passed. Yes, I sat outside in my car. I knew it was God fighting for me. Still, I was stubborn. I am not going back home. I am going to stay the night with him and whatever happens, happens, I am not going to stop it. After that, a car comes, and they had a gate key. So I followed behind the car and parked, the lady was walking into the building, so I said excuse me ma'am my friend ask me to come over, but I think he fell asleep on me. Do you mind if I come into the building behind you? She said, Ok. Now, when I made it to his door, his keys were still in the door. My heart begins to race like what is going on.

I took the keys out of the door and opened it, and he was standing there, and so were 2 Caucasian women. All of the laughings stopped when I walked in the door. I asked him why did he leave me downstairs, why didn't you answer your phone. So, then he walked them out and invited me to come out as well. I just stayed inside. When he came back in he asked me to leave and begin to drag me out, He begins to yank me by my hair and pull me. He said that I embarrassed him in front of his company. I disrespected him. He cannot help where he lives it's not his fault I couldn't get in referring to him residing in an area better than where he felt I lived. He begins to insult me by saying I was an angry black woman, I was uneducated, I was a Single Parent, and nobody wanted me.

I said that is what you think, I had a degree in science and was working on my Business degree. I am divorced, I am not some ghetto black angry single parent. All of these words we were having back and forth before He wrestled me to the ground and began to choke me out. So, as I'm lying on the floor with his hands gripped so tight around my neck to the point of where I couldn't breathe anymore. I had tears rolling down the side of my face as I lay there with my breath taken. I wanted to just to lay there and die. I apparently have learned nothing with all of the celibacy, holiness, and righteousness how did I get back here.

So many thoughts ran through my mind. I asked myself, Dang Girl, DO YOU WANT A RING THAT BAD? I was so Ashamed because I saw how hard God was fighting for me and here I am willing to throw away my salvation, give up celibacy for a man that has ripped out all of my hair and is currently on top of me with his hands gripped around my neck choking the life out of me. I eventually snapped out of the daze gave him a little kick "down there" and threw him off of me. I am a Veteran, so I learned self-defense, and arm to arm combat in the Army. Don't sleep on me now. (Smile) After that, I just asked him to let me get myself together, and I would leave.

When I go to his bathroom and look at myself all I can do is Cry. He pulled out all of my hair and extensions. What killed me on the inside was when I looked and seen THE RING around my Neck. How am I going to explain to everyone why I have this dark red ring around my neck. I guess I got the ring, not the one I wanted, though. I hesitated on sharing this in the book, but I wanted someone to understand that I have been through it because of Impatience. I have suffered some consequences because I was pushing for something that God never desired for my life. I want you to know that I forgave them. We forgave each other. We are great friends. I pray no one feels any way about me sharing my testimony. I have forgiven everyone. I do not hate anyone; I pray that I am forgiven and not hated. God Bless.

Chapter 1

Honesty

Psalm 139:14

praise you because I am fearfully and wonderfully made; your works are wonderful, I know that full well.

You have to allow your relationships to be tested. People could say that it is playing games, but hey you need to know what people are made of, right?. Let me see the real you. Some people will put up a front then they want to take off the mask after they think they have you. No sir, no ma'am. It doesn't work that way. Pay attention to the signs. They are not going to lie. You can't put on a face to get a man or woman then take it off. I don't have the energy for all of that. I agree with being Impressive to a person that you are interested in but not to the point you have a whole

1

new personality outside of who you are inside. I try to be myself as much as possible because I want to scare off as many counterfeits as possible. What happens one day when I want to let my hair down one day and be myself. Will he not like me anymore? What if I go to the movies and I'm the only one Laughing out Loud at a part that wasn't as funny to others. Will he lose interest in me because when I first met him I had a cute little laugh that I practice just for him and now the real me is coming out? I'm a goofball, and my laugh is OUT LOUD.

It's okay to try to impress the person you like but not to the point where you are not yourself, and you are even afraid to be yourself. I would not say drop it all on him at once, but open up and let him see the beauty of the flower that you are inside. There is nothing like being in a relationship where you have pretended so much to be the girl he likes, but it's taking all the joy from you because you are not yourself. The moment you try and let your hair down it's only for a second because he doesn't know this woman, and he doesn't like her. It's not that something is wrong with her it's just not who he fell in love with. Make sure He's falling in love with you and not who you are pretending to be. Maybe who you are isn't quite what he is looking for, and that is fine. All the things he didn't like your man will. Give him the opportunity to love the real you. Be the Best You. Be confident in you. Never try to change for the sake of a man liking you or being interested in you. If you be who you really are you have a better chance of attracting someone that will be compatible with you. Your relationship will be so much smoother when both parties show their real face. All the craziness starts happening when one or the other begin to show their true self. Just be you in the beginning. Give people the opportunity to know what they are getting themselves into. Don't be deceitful.

WHAT YOU WANT ISN'T ALWAYS WHAT YOU NEED

Jeremiah 29:11

For I know the plans I have for you," declares the LORD, "plans to prosper you and not to harm you, plans to give you hope and future.

If you know, this guy is not for you leave him alone. Some may call it a soulish tie, where you connect yourself to someone who God has not purposed for you to become one with. You know what's best for you, but you keep wanting to run back because it is easy, it's comfortable, it's Compromise. You have to fight the feeling, well at least resist the feeling. I believe if we could see the damage that some people do to us internally, spiritually and emotionally, it wouldn't be as hard to move on. We feel it, but we don't see how bad it is for us until it's too late. When we finally decide to leave so much damage has been done you don't know how to begin to heal. You may feel like you are losing, but you're not. Make sure you want what you need because it will bring everything you never knew you wanted. If you know, the Relationship isn't right for you to let it go. Be honest with yourself. I've never seen someone who moved on from a bad situation and regretted it so; you have nothing to lose move forward. Do not ever be afraid of moving forward if there is anything in your past that is meant to be in your future God has no problem with bringing it back around to you. I will never encourage anyone to stay in a bad situation better, yet I will never encourage you to get into a bad situation. If you are ever in that place of trying to decide if you should leave, God will confirm to you what you should do if you ask Him to, He will give you peace in your heart.

MAKE SURE HE WANTS TO CHANGE

James Don't be deceived, my dear brothers and sisters. 1:16

Be careful when you accept people where they are then later you are upset that they don't want to change. You both have to understand that hey this is where I am right now but I want to change and making a conscious effort to do so. You have to know what you can deal with and what you can't deal with in a man. If right now you know something is getting on your nerves, but you like him so, you ignore it because you want to be with him. If you know, you deal with insecurities, and this man is highly handsome why give him a headache. Aim for someone who is a little less attractive maybe (just kidding) If you know you like handsome men look for one who is attractive and humble, attractive and knows his boundaries with women, one who is Godly and attractive.

Every fine guy isn't for you; He is fine, but he wants you and every other woman to know it. Now don't get me wrong he will come with some issues, and that is ok just make sure he is willing to work on them. Some men do not want to change. They want you to take them as is, non-refundable and no warranty and that is a big red flag. The same goes for you too if you know you have some issues you cannot be trying to make the man change to comfort your weakness. If you are dangerously insecure, it doesn't mean he has to close his eyes and turn his head every time he sees a woman you have to become more confident as a woman knowing your relationship is secure in Christ.

FAKING IT UNTIL YOU MAKE IT

Some people do not care about having the real thing especially when they can fake it until they make. As long as I look good, look happy, look like we are happy together; no one has to know the truth about our relationship. The only time the two of you are happy together is when it's in front of people. Husband and Wife who are probably not even living together but you look happy.

You look like what you want people to think. It's time to come out of denial and be real so God can bless you with your true desires. To spend your life pretending, it has to be miserable. It's time for you to be happy for real. It is like people don't want the real thing anymore. How can God bless when everybody is ok with faking, pretending like their Blessed. Let God Bless you this year don't take away His Glory don't settle for the faking. He wants you to have the real thing. Show us that you're still able to do the impossible. I want you to enjoy a real happy relationship. Love has become a fairy tale that some people don't believe can come true. People have become ok with finding something close to it and just put up a front in all the areas that would prove it isn't real. You don't have to fake being happy in a relationship; Real love is out there.

HE'S JUST NOT THE ONE FOR YOU.

Don't force love; it is something that should just happen or something that is built over time. Do not force him to commit or you will have to keep doing that to get him to keep that commitment. Deep down inside a woman doesn't want a man that she had to force to be with her. Don't let him keep running in and out of your life. One minute he wants to settle down the next minute, he doesn't want a commitment. He goes out and plays in the streets then when things do not go as planned he wants to come back home to be a family man. Help him make that decision by closing and locking your door so that he can no longer run in and out of your life. He either wants you or he doesn't. If he is still out there, then let him stay out there. If you both made a commitment to be together, that does not include outsiders. You both have to keep the commitment you made to each other. Never force a man into a relationship with you and restrain him from doing what he wants to do.

I believe if you allow a person to make the commitment make the efforts then your chances are higher with him keeping that promise. Think about when people force you to do things that you do not want to do. You may do it for a while, but eventually, you will rebel in some way. Let his commitment to you be natural. Let it be because you are the only one in his life. Let it be because you are the apple of his eye, the honey to his bun, all of that and some. Never let it be forced. You both will be miserable. Have you ever thought that while you are forcing that man to be with you, your husband is still out there searching for you, but you are caught up in this situation? God has a man out there willing and ready to love you, commit to you, marry you and have a family with you. Stop chasing the men. Stop chasing the men. Stop Chasing men. When a man wants a woman he goes after her and nothing will stop him. He knows how to show his feelings. Don't make another excuse for why he isn't expressing himself, why his actions aren't lining up with his words.

If he was able to show you his feelings when he first made a move on you how did he forget after getting to know you? He knows how to express himself; men know what to do to get a woman, and he knows what it takes. Let go of all the excuses you have made telling yourself this man loves you, but he just doesn't show you his feelings. I don't understand why love is associated more with pain than anything else. It has to hurt you for you to say that it is love. If he loved you the way you want to believe that he does then you would know it, you will feel it. If you are still questioning it, maybe you need to reevaluate it.

I'M SURE HE'S A GOOD MAN BUT IS HE GODS MAN FOR YOU

Make sure that the Good man is God's mans for you. There is someone specific out there for you. You can't pick and choose who you want and make them capable of complimenting you in life. Just because something is good doesn't mean it is for you. You have to pray, say Lord this is a good man but is this whom you have chosen for me? Get pass him being good and make sure he is from God. Don't only ask God about the bad guys ask about the good ones too. Is he the one for me? It is a simple question, but it can make or break your life depending on if you ask or not. Just take the time to seek God concerning the guy you are considering dating. Good isn't always God. Take whoever it is to God. There are many Good Men and Good women in divorce court right now. Think about it.

UNHAPPY RELATIONSHIP = UNHAPPY MARRIAGE

You're unhappy in a relationship, but you're still pressing for the wedding. The only thing marriage will do, have you stuck in an unhappy relationship. After the wedding, you cannot leave you will have no choice but to work it out. You feel that if you can just get the ring on your finger that everything will work itself out. That ring is not your answer and marriage is not the problem solver. Before pressing for a wedding resolve the differences you two have.

The more things you can work out in the relationship the smoother things will flow in the marriage. Use the courtship wisely let the dating process be beneficial. Many people think that happiness is automatically waiting for them after the honeymoon. They believe that there is a significant gift of happiness waiting for them back home after the honeymoon, but it is not. You find joy, love, and peace in your friendship and through that, it creates a happy relationship and a Blessed Marriage.

LET HIM GO IF HE DOESN'T WANT TO STAY

You don't want a man to remain in your life for any other reason than Him wanting to stay. One of the most painful things you can do is run after a man that don't plan on letting you catch him. Be honest with yourself if you have to force someone to be with you how would you feel knowing that it wasn't his choice he is just with you because you forced him.

You hassle him in all of his relationships if he tries to move on from you. You want to let him go, and he is tormented from all of your hell raisings. Is that what you dreamed of, is that the relationship you always wanted. Ask yourself does it hurt more to stay than it does to walk away? Is the temporary pleasure worth a whole lot of pain? It does not have to be like that; there is someone out there who wants to be with just as much as you want to be with him. Wait for him.

NOTHING WILL MAKE THAT WORK

It is not going to work no matter what if he's not the one. If it is not meant to be it will not be. It is just that simple. No matter how much you fast, cry, beg, complain, pray if you have asked God to let His will be done in your life only that will be done. He will not let you chose anybody. No matter what, those relationships are going to keep slipping through your hands. Yes God gives us choices. At the end of the day, it is up to us to choose. If you have surrendered the area of relationships over to God, then trust Him to lead you to the Right man.

DON'T LET YOUR FAITH MESS YOU UP

Sometimes your Faith can mess you up. Faith comes by hearing and hearing by the word of God if you didn't hear God say he was going to do that don't be doing silly things. Even though God can do it, He never told him to do so like seeing a guy with potential just because he has the potential doesn't mean He is the one. You can use your Faith to believe God for something he doesn't want you to have. Just because it is possible doesn't mean that is what God will do. Let's be realistic with what God is doing in your life. You know when your faith is way out there. Your Faith can't be way out there beyond what God has already said He was going to do in your life. Let common sense kick in. Well if God doesn't want me with him he will do this or that. God, if we are meant to be together, allow this to happen or if you don't want us together then do this. God is not going to always go all the way out of His way to perform all of these signs for you. When He knows, and you know, the answer is and was a no from the door.

Chapter 2

Breaking Cycles

Isaiah 43:19

Behold, I will do a new thing; now it shall spring forth; shall ye not know it? I will even make a way in the wilderness, and rivers in the desert.

Sometimes you have to come out of familiarity and into the unknown to experience what you have never experienced before; don't just step out of your comfort zone, come all the way out of your comfort zone. That is when you will find yourself in the zone, Your Element being who you have always wanted to be and doing what you've always wanted do with who you want to do it with. Has the thought ever crossed your mind to try something new? If who you have been dating, the types you have been dating has been leading you to the same results. Why not try a different type?

13

How about changing the locations you go to all the time? Instead of going to Walmart try shopping at Target.

Change your scenery, change spots, try a new random park, a new restaurant, a new mall, join a new sport, hang out with new friends. There are so many different things you can do to get a better chance to run into the guy of your dream. Just think of the places you have met some of the guys it should have given you a huge clue of what you may be getting yourself into by dealing with him. If he pulled beside you at the red light in a family van with two car seats in the back, come on now you know this man probably has some serious baby momma drama or perhaps a Married-Family man.

Pay attention to these things. You decided to go out to a club, your girls said let's get you out of the house so you can meet someone but the club, really? You may get what the world calls lucky and run into a guy who never goes out he's in a similar situation as you who just happened to come out of the house by one of his boys. Like I said, you may get lucky but for the unlucky ones what you see is what you get. You can't meet him in the club start dating him and expect him to stay at home and watch movies with you every Saturday night. No, he loves the party scene and likes to stay turned up, or lit as they say. No ladies, no and please be careful about church too because what you see isn't always what you get. Some people come to church just to get a good godly Christian woman why because he wants someone who is faithful and he doesn't have to worry about where she is at while he is out doing his thing. Outside of that your location and the situation you met him in play a huge role in the character he has a man, not in every case but do pay attention to where you met him.

DON'T MISTREAT THE GOOD GUY

It is crazy when you find someone that loves you and not playing Games you start thinking something is wrong with the guy. Now you're the one playing games. Don't become the one that begins the game playing. Have you ever found yourself ignoring calls, ignoring the text, sending sorry I was busy messages? Be upfront don't be misleading. Don't have the good guy chasing you while you are chasing the wrong guy. Think about how it feels to be played to the left don't do it to the guy who is making the extra effort to treat you like a Queen. I don't understand why a high percent of women like to be the aggressors. It is a man's job to pursue you. I am sure there are plenty of stories of women who initiated things with their mate or now husband and things have turned out well for them. That is a blessing, but that is not everyone's testimony. Don't try to exercise all of your standards on the right guy and even make the rules harder and higher for the guy you don't want but throw your standards completely out of the window for a guy that you do want but don't need.

LET HIM BE YOUR LAST MISTAKE

You've failed for the Okie-doke far too many times. How many more times will you fall for the same type of guy? You keep telling God you learned from the last time but after he heals you-you go right back to what broke you down in the first place. Do you not believe that there is someone out there for you? Why keep repeating the same cycles?

You fixed yourself up from the last relationship and you ready to do it again but you end up picking up right where you left off. Let him be your last mistake if you are learning what you are supposed to be learning from the errors; you wouldn't repeat them. You may be changing some things that you did, but you are still getting the same results. It could be because you did not pinpoint what it was that God wanted you to learn. Just because you are changing things, it doesn't mean things are going to change. You have to change the right things to get the expected results. Pray and ask God to reveal to you exactly why the cycle is repeating in your life and after he does make the necessary adjustments.

BETTER THAN YOUR LAST ONE

He comes doing more than what the last guy did now you claim him as being a good man but just give it time. You have to see him for who he is give him time. He may not be a good man he just may be better than the last one you had. Take a moment and make sure that he is the best man for you. Don't settle for him being better than the one you just got out of a relationship with letting him be everything you have been waiting on. You can't keep finding men that are better than this one, and this one is better than that one, and this one is better than both of them. Don't do that. Choose the best one. Just because he is doing a little bit more than the last one does not mean he is doing his best. It doesn't mean he is the best he's just better than the last one.

THE SAME TYPE OF GUY

What are you attracting? Why do you keep drawing the same kind of people? You pull to needy people because of your need to be wanted. You figure if they need you then they will want you but sometimes it just ends up with them getting what they want and leaving you in need. What are you drawing is Like Spirits? It's like him needing a place to stay and you having a house. The opposite is drawing, but the fact that you are both in need is bringing you to each other. Sometimes you can pull to people based off of the internal issues you both have in your lives. The negative things that you both have within you have attracted you to each other. Just because the vibe is strong and feels good, it doesn't mean that it is a good thing. Be able to know yourself in the midst of knowing yourself you will be able to recognize what is in others. Learn yourself and Break old patterns and bad habits.

Chapter 3

Love

WHAT YOU WANT ISN'T ALWAYS WHAT YOU NEED

Jeremiah 29:11

For I know the plans I have for you," declares the LORD, "plans to prosper you and not to harm you, plans to give you hope and future.

If you know, this guy is not for you leave him alone. Some may call it a soulish tie, where you connect yourself to someone who God has not purposed for you to become one with. You know what's best for you, but you keep wanting to run back because it is easy, it's comfortable, it's Compromise. You have to fight the feeling, well at least resist the feeling. I believe if we could see the damage that some people do to us internally, spiritually and emotionally, it wouldn't be as hard to move on. We feel it, but we don't see how bad it is for us until it's too late. When we finally decide to leave so much damage has been done you don't know how to begin to heal. You may feel like you are losing, but you're not. Make sure you want what you need because it will bring everything you never knew you wanted.

If you know, the Relationship isn't right for you to let it go. Be honest with yourself. I've never seen someone who moved on from a bad situation and regretted it so; you have nothing to lose move forward. Do not ever be afraid of moving forward if there is anything in your past that is meant to be in your future God has no problem with bringing it back around to you. I will never encourage anyone to stay in a bad situation better, yet I will never encourage you to get into a bad situation. If you are ever in that place of trying to decide if you should leave, God will confirm to you what you should do if you ask Him to, He will give you peace in your heart.

HE WILL SPOT YOU OUT OF THE BUNCH

Ruth 2:5

Then said Boaz unto his servant that was set over the reapers, Whose damsel (young woman) is this?

I want To Encourage My Single Saved Sanctified Women of God. I know you're waiting to be Found by a Mighty Man of God...But Understand although they get to choose the Woman...you have the choice of Who you're Chosen By. Don't Be an Option. You Don't have To Settle. Remember Our Price is Far Above Rubies. While they are Nick picking through the Bunch...YOUR TRUE KING WILL SPOT YOU OUT OF THE BUNCH. Don't worry about other women. If he is yours, Trust me He will Recognize you. You don' have to sound a siren. Blow the horn. Do Tricks. Wave a Flag. If you are his...He will Know it is you. Remember He has been looking for you. I don't care if there are a million look-alikes that man will know the details of who you are why because He prayed for you. And there you stand with all of what he asked for. Don't worry; He will Know you, I don't care who is on his face. He will be drawn to you Beyond any pull another woman could have on him. What God has for you. It's Yours.

A KING WILL TREAT YOU LIKE A QUEEN

Proverbs 31:10

Who can find a virtuous woman? For her price is far above rubies.

With a Price as Far as Rubies, I Deserved the Best not Desperate at all won't settle for anything less, no longer in the world, so I don't accept mess, if you want to be the Priest, then I'm going to put you the test, wherever your heart is at it will manifest. If you are being treated any less than a Queen, then you might need to check the throne. Who do you have sitting in the Kings Seat? Just because You placed him there doesn't make Him a King. You can't make him into one. Wait for God to fill that seat. That king will know just how to handle his Queen. It comes automatic. A King and Queen work hand and hand. They flow together. You can't choose anyone to be King. You can't make him a King if He wasn't born to be one. Anything less than a King is unfit for a Queen.

LOVING WITHOUT LIMITS

1 peter 4:8

Above all, love each other deeply, because love covers over a multitude of sins.

Do you think you can love without limitations or will every man be held to what you have been experienced? Each relationship deserves a fresh slate. Remember this guy has not done anything wrong to you. He deserves a chance. Now, I didn't say be foolish. Please use the wisdom from past experiences but please do not make him pay for anyone else mistake. Treat every relationship as so, don't pick up right where you left off with the last person. You can't keep moving on and moving forward with the open wounds of your past. Clean yourself up; heal, so that you can be ready for another relationship.

JUST ROLL WITH HIM

You'll never know what God is doing just Roll with Him. Sometimes it is hard to figure out what God is up to but don't get ahead of him. Don't jump the gun. Don't downplay or underestimate what He is doing either. Just lay back and enjoy the ride. When you enter a relationship with a guy, don't be crazy anxious trying to figure out where is it going because sometimes your anxiety can cause him to back off. Relax and just enjoy good company. When you allow the relationship to grow naturally, you end up having the best friendships.

Things just come and flow naturally. Please relax I know you had it all planned out. You knew what you would do, what you would say but then God switched things up. He blessed you while you were not expecting it, with someone you didn't expect it with so now you have to trust him on how to manage the blessing. You can't pour old wineskins into new wineskins or else it will burst. Your old plan isn't going to work for the new thing God is doing in your life. Just go with God's flow.

THE RIGHT HANDS OF THE RIGHT MAN

God will not place you in the hand of any man He must know what to do with you. You need a leader. Women you need a man who can lead you. There's a difference in Him wanting you to be submissive just so he can do whatever he want to do and in him wanting you to trust and submit because he has you, he got you. I believe in being submissive but let me give you an example. Let's say the relationship was a car the man is in control driving the vehicle, but he is driving crazy running red lights, Don't stop at stop signs, swerving in and out of lanes.

As a woman, you would be afraid to let this man drive you. The same for a relationship or marriage no woman wants to be in a relationship with a man who is making reckless decisions. You want to feel safe, protected, cared for, and thought of in the process of his decision making. So allow God to put you in the hands of the right man. A man that will make decisions based on what is best for the both of you.

A MAN WILL KNOW HOW TO TREAT YOU.

If he is a man, a God sent man. He will know exactly how to handle you, how to handle you, how to talk to you and take care of you. Anything less than that you will always be pumping and priming him to love you. Everybody may not be fortunate enough to be blessed with one who knows exactly what to do, but I can guarantee you that if he is God sent he will be willing to learn what to do. Every guy won't see you for who you are God will allow them to see you wrong, he won't allow him to see you so that he can hide you from the wrong one so that the one can find you. The one will see you in all of your splendor and all of your Glory. No need to convince a man of all that you are just be you.

PREPARING FOR MARRIAGE

No one is ever really ready for marriage. We get as prepared as we can. We go into it with the mindset that I'm willing to do whatever it takes to make it work but what about when you don't feel like that anymore? How about the one you all say, love; we love each other. The truth is not even loving can keep some people together. That's just truth. You need more than love to make a marriage last. You need patience humility forgiveness.

A lot of individuals who love each other still got a divorce. Think about it. You need more than love for marriage. You need the Lord. You need a strong foundation a pure Love, Respect, Understanding, and Patience. No matter how much you prepare and practice you are still going to need God to guide you in marriage to keep you in marriage. Keep practicing but know it will still be a learning process.

Chapter 4

Mistakes

WHEN YOU RUSH, YOU MISS STUFF

Philippians 4:6

Be anxious for nothing, but in everything by prayer and supplication with thanksgiving let your requests be made known to God.

e anxious for nothing but everything by prayer and supplication. I have learned to take my time in dating because I would take a guy on everything he says out of his mouth no matter if he ever did any of it or not. As bad as you would want to fall madly in love with this guy, DON'T. Take your time. Pay attention to the Details. If not you will be 4-5 months or even years into a mess when it could have been avoided. When you first meet a person, you may not know them, but the details will show you who they are if you are paying attention. When things don't sit well with you, then it's probably not well. Be wise. What's happening now is the Lie is being established in the beginning, so that you will not question them in the end.

Example. He doesn't answer the phone after a certain time at night. In the beginning, he told you he worked two jobs one in the day and one in the evening. So, he will hit you up now and then at night but don't want you to get comfortable with calling at night. Another example is He only text you. There is always a reason he can't call. When the timing is too perfect, pay attention to that; bring him out of his routine if he always calls or wants to see you at certain times or a certain day pay attention to that. Switch up the days. If he wants to see you on Wednesday, say Wednesday is not okay. How about Thursday? Or How about Saturday at 3:00 p.m. Got them.

If he can't be too flexible with his time or days of the week, pay attention to that. Of course men have lives, work, gym, hanging with the guys but still watch out for these signs. The thing is he is not trying to get you use to something he won't be able to keep up. So he fixes it before it even becomes a problem. If he told you, he has a night job. You're not going to question why he never answers his phone at night. If he says, in the beginning, I don't like talking on the phone, you won't question why he is always texting. I don't want you to be all paranoid because every guy is not like that but I tell you so that you can watch and pray. Pay attention to what signs you see. They have gotten wiser and so should you.

HOW CAN SOMETHING SO RIGHT BE SO WRONG?

1 corinthians 14:40

Let's get rid of this whole side-chick thing. Side chick means that his election is not sure. He will just rather flip a coin. If the side-chick leaves, I still got my main woman. If my main woman leaves, then my side-chick is still there. He is good either way. Neither woman has the dignity to say, hey, this is intolerable. I deserve a man who will only have eyes for me; a man that can make and keep a commitment to me. Ladies I do know it is possible to fall in love with someone who is in a relationship. Usually, you don't found out until you have feelings already. That's the catch to it.

They get you to fall in love first after you have all types of feelings for them then the truth starts leaking out because now you are demanding more of his time. You are calling more frequently, and he has to begin to lie harder or even start opening you up to the truth because if he doesn't, he is a phone call or two away from you catching him up on his double life. He has played with your feelings now you are ready to break up his home or whatever he has going on because he only came and toyed with your heart. It is very heartbreaking. The other woman is considered the homewrecker. Some great women get caught in those types of situation. I encourage you not to get stuck. You're going to have to be a big girl and reel your feelings in because that kind of drama you do not need in your life. Even if you get him all to yourself your trust will be damaged, and you will always have in the back of your mind will he do the same thing to me. If he leaves her for me will he leave me for another? How you start how you usually finished the same way. Always try your best to start your relationship off the right way, in decency, and in order. Laying the right things in your foundation is necessary. What you are building on plays a huge role in whether or not it will last.

WHAT ABOUT SEX?

Mark 10:8

"And the two will become one flesh.' So they are no longer two, but one flesh."

You have to understand that when you are having sex with someone you are becoming one with their flesh. You are becoming one person. So think about that the next time you lay down with someone.

Sex and Saints is a hot topic discussion. Is it wrong is it ok? Can I "M-Bate" how can I refrain and maintain celibacy? This subject right here along with other conversations can be very touchy. So, I'm just going to give my opinion, if that is okay? I believe that "Sex can Wait." The danger of having sex before marriage is that you can get drawn into someone solely based off of the GOOD SEX. The sex was good, but he was in a relationship with someone else. The sex was good, but he hits you every now and again. The sex was good, and you don't care if he ever gets a job because the way he makes love to you drives you insane. Yes, insane is the right word.

Do not be crazy, falling in love, getting married because you had Good sex with someone. When that Sex wears off, and bills start rolling in, when that sex wears off, and now you are getting boring to him, he wants something new. What do you guys have to stand on other than what you built the relationship of? Good sex can't pray for you. Good sex isn't a Good father. Good sex doesn't want to go to church. Good sex won't get a Job. So, ask yourself what did Good sex get you into?

If some of your sex life went sour right now, nothing would be holding your relationship/marriage together. I'm not going to be unrealistic and say that it is the easiest thing in the world to do because it is not. It is extremely hard to do, but with God, a good support group or good friend to confide in will be very helpful throughout the process. To be honest, you will make some mistakes; He is going to be so Fine, Vibes So Strong and you're going to find it hard to resist. I'm not saying everyone is going to fall some people make it through God's grace and some people fall and only get back up by God's grace nevertheless everyone will make it through somehow by God's grace.

For so many years I used an accountability system even though before that I chose to live my life in a way that I believed to be honorable to God, so the accountability system was just an extra cushion. I would never be alone with a guy in private places; it would have to be a very public event or a group outing. That was good however it doesn't matter how many systems you use the decisions is left up to you to do what you believe is right. I believe by waiting you have stronger friendship and lasting respect. Respect does go out of the window in some aspect after sex. Jealousy and all types of other things ease into the relationship, and it's harder to finish developing a foundation because both parties flesh has taken over. It's hard to develop something Spiritual in the Flesh.

I will just encourage you to wait as long as you can the better your relationship will be. I know some people have no problem with resisting sex because they have their alternate M-Bating or toys. I'm not going to get into that. I will just say try your best to refrain from entertaining those sexual desires. Continuous Prayer fasting and reading of the word will help you to overcome those desires. It is a one step at a time thing. The only thing I can suggest other than that just grab a pillow and say help me Lord help me. The Lord has put me to sleep plenty of nights. I said Lord just please get me through the night, and in the midst of me praying I always fall into a deep sleep and wake up the next morning Strong and Victorious. Just be as patient as you can God wants to help us with these things and he will if we allow Him to. Side note: Don't ever pray for your desire for sex to go away. Then end up married and wonder what happened to your desire for sex. Pray Lord, Give me self-control until my husband come; help me to hold out until my wedding reception is over Father. (Smile)

AFTER YOU ATTRACT HIM WILL YOUR CHARACTER KEEP HIM

Ecclesiastes 4:12

And if someone overpowers one person, two can resist him. A cord of three strands is not easily broken.

Whatever you do to get a man you will have to continue that to keep him. So be careful what you do to get him because you have to do the same thing to keep him. If showing off your body, being lustful is attracting him to you congratulations you just won yourself a lifetime of being seductive just to keep his attention, and I feel sorry for you when he runs into the one who is just a little more seductive than you are then there go his focus and your relationship. You have to have something that every woman doesn't have something Godly that every woman does not possess. If your price isn't far above Rubies, then you don't have worth. Have something that is God given that will keep his attention. Let your prayer life be on point give him things any, and every woman can't give him. Don't manipulate to get him you will get tired of turning tricks to keep him. Just be who God has called you to be. Let it be the things of the Spirit that keep him drawn to you anything else that draws him won't keep him fascinated long. Let God be that thing that has him drawn and all in love.

Don't to share your love life with everyone especially with other single women. If you are friends, it is likely be so quick you both will have the same or similar taste in men. So at some point you will probably be crushing on the same guy. The enemy is slick, whenever he sees something about to transpire in your life, he will send people to block it. Especially in the church as I was saying before about how many women will put dibs on one man. God can have someone specific for you, but then the enemy will send an assignment what do I mean by assignment, he will send one who is interested in the guy to you. Now they are confiding in you about the guy, and you have become stuck because out of all the people why would she come to you. Now there is a conflict of interest because you don't want to seem like you betrayed her when in reality the enemy sent the person to throw you off. Everybody that comes to you with a smile shouldn't be embraced. I do not encourage bickering over men, however when God is preparing to send your mate that is not the time to be trying to make new friend girls. Keep it less complicated. No new friends. Smile.

BAD RELATIONSHIP ADVISERS

You can't expect someone in a bad relationship to advise you on how to get into a good one. They have made a bad relationship choice, and you see that but yet and still you are getting their opinion on what God has for you. They can't give you what they don't have. How can they tell you if you have a good man or not if the one they have isn't good? Be careful with who you are confiding and getting your advice from. You will be amazed at some of the twisted advice people will give you. You have people that are jealous and don't want to see you with anyone. So they will constantly be trying to keep you single. Find someone Godly with wisdom and have your best interest at heart. Let God lead you to the person or people you can get legit advice from, someone who will speak from the heart of God, not out of their knowledge or perception of you and past situations.

YOU ARE TOO OLD TO BE STILL CREEPING

Do not sneak around trying to get a little something-something on the low. Sometimes that will backfire on you. I encourage everyone to stop answering the late night text and calls; you know the ones that say Hey are you up? Where are you you? Wyd? Are you coming to see me? Ignore them, as a matter of fact; those numbers shouldn't even be in the call log anymore, but you want to save a number just in case. You do not need a just in case delete that number block it if you have to.

Listen it defeats the purpose if you remove the number after you spent a few days memorizing it. I have been there a few times, hitting that delete button with no problem but then that message pops up "Are you sure you want to Delete" it will get you every time. Or either you'll delete it knowing he is going to call, you are still on his Facebook account, still following him on Instagram, got his email, his mother house number. Deleting that number isn't helping you, you are fooling yourself. Quit playing with it. You can get burned if you continue to play with fire. Try to refrain from things that will tempt you.

GET YOURSELF BACK TOGETHER

So you fell in Love with someone who keeps hurting you? It's Simple Stand back up and get yourself back together. How much longer are you going to go through with this guy? I understand that it hurts. I understand that he did you wrong but when will you bounce back from this? If he had a love for you the way, you believed He would not have put you through the process you have to go through right now. I am not saying that every relationship is supposed to be perfect, but please know what the limits are; please understand when it needs to be cut off. If you are at the place where you cannot eat, sleep or breathe without this man, there is a significant problem. Has this person become your Idol?

You should only feel that way about God. When a man or woman becomes an Idol that is when God will move them out of the way. The heart of the King is in God's hands, and He will turn it which every way He pleases. So, if God wanted him to be with you he would be, He can easily touch his heart to come back to you but why hasn't he done that? You have to get to the point where everything other than God is secondary. Don't bring yourself down so low when a man walks out. It's easier said than done, but with God it is possible. It took me years to get over my divorce, and I'm not talking about the love I had for him but ten years to get over the pain I suffered physically mentally and emotionally. I lost myself in my ex-husband. I lost myself in him way before I was married to him. I lived and breathed him. Loving him was killing me. I was so damaged, broken and torn, mentally shattered. I almost lost my mind because I couldn't process the pain. God sent an angel to say to me, if you don't pull yourself together you will lose everything. After that piece by piece, I gathered myself, my thoughts, and whatever was left of my emotions and have been taking it one step and one day at a time. Trust me if I can do it you can too. I didn't tell you the whole story, just know that no matter what you can get yourself back together Stronger and better than before.

LEARN TO KEEP IT MOVING

If I haven't learned anything else about life, I've learned to keep it moving. Another hard thing to do is keep it moving when you know God has shut a door, and you know there is no coming back from it. As much as you want to keep knocking, keep believing that one day God will reopen that door, you have to have the courage to walk away. Whenever God shuts a door, it is saying Move on. It's only hard to leave when you do not know the possibilities that God has in store for you. Believe past what you currently see. As many feelings and time you have put into that situation, it feels like a waste, but God will fill you back up and restore the time you feel you lost in that relationship. Understand there is so much more in store for you. God has better than your Best. You have to be Strong mentally tough enough to make a common sense decision. Yes, I made that word up. Our heart will have us out there bad. We will love someone to life and back. God has given us a heart like that. Use them both let them give each other Balance needed to make a decision that is best for you.

NO NEED TO BE EMBARRASSED

One door closed means another one is opening. I remember speaking with a relationship class instructor. I was embarrassed to tell her that my last relationship failed and that I was now with a new guy attending the class. She said, I should not be embarrassed. The most embarrassing thing is being with the wrong person. That is what's embarrassing. Which lets me know that meant that there are a lot of people who will keep pressing in the wrong relationship just to be in one. So, what she was saying was yes people might look at you or even say things concerning the fact that you were dating this guy and now you are dating this guy, that's why it's good not to sleep around. It's easier to move on dating is the process of determining whether the person is right for you. Don't be embarrassed, getting it right is all that matters.

THREE IS STILL A CROWD

Keep your friends out of your business. Relationships mixed with Friendships three is a crowd. What happens most of the time is you end up talking to them about your problems, and the problems consist of all the things that are wrong with the man making him seem like a bad guy when in reality he is a pretty good guy but you are only focusing on the issue at hand.

Therefore you only discuss the negative things. So, you will hear the girl leave him, no I will not deal with that, girl let him go, then before the clock strikes midnight you and him are back together, and now your girl can't stand him because of all of the bad things you have said. That's why I would suggest just take it to the king, tell God about your situation. Get instructions, and deal with your issues but I don't agree with getting family and friends involved.

There will be some disagreements maybe even some arguing in your relationship but once you have put a bad taste in your family's mouth for the man you love it's hard to wash that taste out of their mouth. So if it's not life or death quit dialing everyone up telling them what's wrong with your man because they will not say anything about the issues the are having with their man in which half of the time is way worst. So keep your business to yourself. Learn to talk it out with him more than you talk about him to your friends.

THEY GOT TO GET CLOSE ENOUGH TO YOU TO GET TO HIM

Be careful do not bring every friend into your relationship. People will talk you out of your Blessing, and the whole time they wanted it. They're hoping it slips right out of your hands into theirs. You cannot even bring some family into your relationship. For better words don't be crazy about it but you know the ones you wouldn't trust to even blink your eyes around them. They send out signals and vibes to your boyfriend or husband. Don't be overly suspicious because that is not a good look on you, my queen. Even if you have a man that is super trustworthy don't set him up for failure at the end of the day we are all human. Don't leave him in the room with Ms. Jezebel or whatever her name may be. There is a way to do everything you cannot be insecure but do be wise. Other women can smell insecurity because most women can be insecure or have been at some point in their life. If you are single, do not have a man with you do not make hanging around other couples a habit, be respectful. I don't hang around anybody and their man. I even give my mom and dad respect and privacy. That's how deep it is for me. Dress appropriately. If you know your Boobs are out, you shouldn't be leaning all over so your shirt can fall more and reveal more. Women can do some slick untrustworthy stuff. Some do it unaware, but most know what they are doing. As a woman, you shouldn't be trying to provoke someone else's, man. Eventually when you get one trust me, one day one will come to provoke yours.

If a man ever fell for that trick, he would never trust you around another man because he knows what you are capable of doing when his back is turned. If you wouldn't want it done to you, do not do it to someone else. Thank you.

Chapter 5

Knowledge

WHEN THE RELATIONSHIP BLOWS UP IN YOUR FACE

Proverbs 16:9

We can make our plans, but the LORD determines our steps.

You may be asking yourself why do relationships blow up directly in your face? Things could be going extremely well, and out of nowhere, things would drastically change. You are like, what did I do? You are evaluating yourself and saying, maybe I was calling too much, or maybe I should have let him text first. Maybe I was getting on his nerves. Maybe I was a little too pushy. Maybe I was pressuring him. Maybe I was too aggressive. Let me stop you there. You did nothing wrong to the point where it would make a man just rudely and abruptly lose interest in a relationship with you. There could be a billion reasons of why, when it comes to the things he has or had going on in his life that you know nothing about. What went wrong was, that was not the particular situation God intended for you or the special person God has for you. God wants to demonstrate his love for you through man. Therefore, he would not send someone in your life to tear you apart. That is the enemies doing, and you have to be the one to say no. There is nothing wrong with me this situation is just not right for me.

GOD IS NOT OBLIGATED TO BRING TO PASS WHAT YOU WANT

Psalm 37:4

Take delight in the LORD, and he will give you the desires of your heart.

I'm getting married next year; I'm going to be a millionaire before I turn 40, God this is my last year being broke, etc., then it doesn't happen, and now you're questioning God, about why He didn't come through. And the answer is you told Him that He didn't tell you that. God never makes a Promise that He Won't Keep. Don't confuse His Promise with what you want and what you have said. God is only obligated to bring to pass what He has promised you. Not what you have told him you wanted and when you want him to do it. Stop placing demands on God. Ask God to show you His will and pray that His will be done. That is how you get what you want when it lines up with what He wants for you. Let your desires be His desires, and you will have them. God can bless us way better than we can bless ourselves. Trust that what He wants for you is the Best for you.

YOU HAVE TO CHANGE FIRST

Ephesians 5:20

Giving thanks always for all things to God and the Father in the name of our Lord Jesus Christ;

You know I Kept hoping for things to get better but they kept getting worse and I realize that in the process of Things Getting Worse I am getting better. I realized that things weren't designed to change, but things were designed for me to change. So, I'm just going to do it. You cannot expect for everything to change in your life to be happy. Let the change start with how you feel about yourself and the things you go through in life. The greatest project you can work on is yourself. As you begin to make a difference in your habits, things may still be the same, but the way you look at them will be so much more different. And it will have less adverse effects on you and your life in general. True happiness comes from within you. You cannot expect (the nouns) people, places or things to bring happiness. Once you are happy with your life, the people the places and things will eventually line up. I can almost promise you that more of the things that bring you joy will come. You will begin to attract more things to make you happy. You will start to attract beautiful things in your life. Maybe the reason you are attracting or drawing things that are not making you happy is that you are not satisfied inside. Try appreciating life. Try finding more things that put a smile on your face. More things will begin to fill your life. Just like they say when a man is appreciated and complimented he starts to do more things to make you happy or smile. The same things happen in life, the more you enjoy life it blesses you with more beautiful things and greater experiences. God is the same. He loves to be complimented and appreciated. Thank him more for what He has done already, and He will bless you beyond your imagination.

HE SPEAKS TO YOUR HEART

Proverbs 3:5

Trust in the LORD with all your heart and lean not on your understanding;

Most times when you are in need of direction or an answer to your prayer, you wait on God to speak to you through outside sources, give a sign, give you a prophecy, but for the most part, He speaks to your heart. If you're asking to be in His will understand that He placed His will in your heart. Correct your heart can be deceitful, but that's when we talk about the emotions that you follow that cannot be trusted. He gave you the wisdom to determine what is of you and what is of Him. The Holy Spirit will lead you into all Truth. Meaning you may not see your answer right away but if you will move and trust that nudging inside of you. You may not get an answer before you make a move, making a move will give you the answer. Hope seen is not hope at all. Who hopes for what they can see? The just shall live by faith. We are not exempt from making mistakes, but we're expected to Trust God in every step we take and every move we make. If God has spoken to you concerning a matter, He may not keep confirming what He has already said to you. If we tell a child to do something and you know they heard you would you keep repeating yourself? Probably not. We can't expect God to talk to us through the entire process you can't be Afraid to move off of what He has said. Peter asked, Lord if it's you bid me to come and he stepped out of the Boat. Maybe if Jesus had talked to Him every step of the way, Peter wouldn't have begun to sink. Stop second guessing yourself and be sure of what He said. Just because we never move on the Word doesn't mean God never said it. We just never moved on it. His word never changes we don't act on the word then say that's not what God had for me. He's Gentle, He won't force you, and after a while, He eventually stops nudging you. I encourage you to Trust in the Lord with all thine heart and all thy soul and lean not on your own understanding, in all your ways acknowledge Him, and He Shall Direct your Path. I want God to bless you with the Desires of your heart so listen for His voice as you make steps of Faith.

KEEP THIS IN MIND

Matthew 7:7

Ask, and it will be given to you; seek, and you will find; knock, and the door will be opened to you.

God won't make available to you what He doesn't want you to have, and He won't make Unavailable to you what He wants you to have. Stop knocking on old closed doors and walk through the New Doors He has opened do not stress out over doors that will close or have closed. If God wants you to walk through them, He will make away for you. If it is for you, it will be yours. No need to beat down the door. When it is of God as you walk up to it, the door will be open for you. The word of God does say knock, and the door will be open unto you. That door is heaven's door, when you knock on heaven's door, the door God has for you will pop open. Don't let your knock be more for what you want than it is for God.

HOW YOU START YOU WILL FINISH

Ecclesiastes 7:8

The end of matter is better than its beginning, and patience is better than pride.

The thing about starting on the down low with a man is that you may never come out. Be upfront about the courtship. I do believe in keeping your dating life somewhat hidden meaning everyone doesn't have to know. But it shouldn't have to be a secret. Some guys do not want the relationship out in the open so that there is no accountability in it. If he is serious about you, then He shouldn't mind being open with dating you. Some guys like to stay behind the scenes so that he could possibly date multiple girls at one time, not in all cases but some cases it is true.

I did say already keep the relationship somewhat private the people that should know are people that can benefit the relationship as far as wisdom, prayers, and guidance. Before a relationship or courtship goes public make sure there is something concrete there. You do not want to be quick to let everyone know then it doesn't work out now you are with someone else, and people are just confused at what is going on with your dating life. I do not care what the reasons were for dating different people back to back it never looks good to the general public. It just seems like you have been with a lot of guys in a short period. It doesn't matter if you didn't sleep together it is just a negative image overall. I would suggest just getting to know a person before you consider it a courtship. Call it someone I'm getting to know. I know dating is the process of getting to know someone, but there are some things you can find out in casual conversation that will let you know if he is a person that you should consider dating. That will save you from dating multiple guys. Before you enter the dating process, just have casual conversations and in that process decide if you would like to date him. We get so excited that we just want to rush the entire process. We just met, now we are going on our first date. Be careful don't be quick to go out on a date. Have general conversation first. A lot can be washed out through those conversations. Just slow down the process, and you will save yourself a couple of break ups and messed up friendships. Some people you are called to be friends with for Kingdom purposes, but we feel a little tingle now we're trying to date them. Slow down and ask God, what is the purpose of meeting this guy? Every man you meet isn't for you to date. There are plenty people I have met initially off of attraction, but it wasn't for courtship or marriage it was for ministry or business purposes. Take the time find out why you two are drawing together.

TRUE COLORS

Ephesians 5:13

But all things being exposed by the light are made evident.

When a person is always finding a reason to get upset with you or get upset with you real quick over small things. You may want to pay very close attention to that because truth is they have been feeling some way. But we are in a time where true colors will always shine through; no longer will it hide behind a smile. If he loves you it will show if he does not like you: you will know. His actions will tell you just how he feels about you. Some guys are just different they express themselves in various ways; it all depends on the upbringing and habits picked up along the way. Pay attention to what God is showing you. He is highlighting it for a reason. He makes it plain as day for you. What you see in some cases may not be what it is but in most cases it is made plain as day to you after you pray Watch.

THEY THINK DIFFERENT

Romans 12:9

Love must be sincere

Women you have to understand that Men think entirely different than we think. They don't function the way we function. They don't respond the way we respond. You may believe he doesn't love you, but he could be madly in love with you. You can't determine how a man feels about you based on him replicating the same way you expressed your love to him. We want them to understand us but have you tried learning him. Every man doesn't show love through buying you gifts and spending a lot of time with you. But look at what he does, when he's with you, the man may open up and bring you into his personal space, the place where he spends all his time. In which, he may have never done before, and it's his way of showing you how much you mean to him.

That's why it is so important to get to know each other and learn each other's love language. Learn His ways. We cannot expect them to show love the same way we do. They are different. First of all, they are a different person from who we are secondly they are men we are women two entirely different ways of doing things. Instead of seeing it that way, we call him a liar; accuse him of doing the same thing with other females, etc. And you end up killing the vibe, the love he was developing for you. You have to let him love you naturally; too many times things are forced therefore it doesn't work. Love me like this, Love me like that; I didn't know love came with instructions!?! You may be missing out because if you let him love you the way he wants, He may love you in a way you could not imagine.

MEN SETTLE TOO

Proverbs 18:22

He who finds a wife finds what is good and receives favor from the LORD.

Don't think because he chose someone else to marry that you are anything less than the best because men settle too. You may be thinking the person was better than you prettier than you etc. when the truth is a man has a choice just like you do. If you chose to settle for less than what God has for you, it doesn't mean he didn't have better it means that you made your choice. The same thing goes for men when he chooses who he wants to marry it doesn't matter if you could have possibly been the better choice. His choice is His choice that doesn't take anything away from who you are as a woman.

You have to understand that sometimes men don't know their worth. Sometimes they settle too. Sometimes they choose the wrong woman just like we sometimes choose the bad guy. They aren't exempt from making mistakes or choosing wrong. They just handle it differently than we do. Even if a guy messes up, he will never admit it. He will act like he has the best thing in the world even if he has to go home and knock himself upside the head. Kick himself in the butt. You will never see that part of it. So do not be fooled they settle too. Just because he finds a woman to marry doesn't mean he found a wife. You will know what he has by whether he Obtained favor or not. Some men go through hell and end up with no favor because of who they chose to walk beside them. They choose by flesh more often than they do by Spirit.

HIS FLAWS

Sometimes we take the flaws too seriously. You have to be mindful that people are nervous and trying to impress you and may do something completely silly that turns you off, but truth is it was out of character for them. You're going to get flaws. There's no getting around that you just have to figure out which ones you are willing to put up with and which ones you can tolerate. You will not be able to get away from flaws. We always find something wrong especially when he is not physically what we were praying and asking for. The first thing we are going to be attracted to is physical attributes of course, but after the initial attraction, the first thing to look for is character traits. Character traits are so important.

How many times have you been interested in a handsome guy but after times pass you realized he is too into himself. It doesn't matter how handsome he is the fact that he is extremely conceited has turned you off. Character traits are important. So many people will choose a good looking person knowing their character is not that good, but they would rather have someone to look good within public and deal with all the bad and the ugly behind the scenes. Be honest with yourself when it comes to what you can handle. Remember if you marry this person that thing will be what you will have to live with so make sure it is something you can deal for the rest of your life.

GUYS CAN BE VERY INDECISIVE

Men can be double minded. They will forget that they were pursuing you. They won't remember they were trying to be with you. It is hard to understand a man who will pursue you like crazy then try to reverse the roles and act like you are sweating them. You don't blow them up; you don't stalk them, give them space, and they say you don't ever call me. You don't ever want to chill with me or go out with me but when you start to do all those things.

They act as if you are trying to force them into a relationship. Wait didn't you ask me to do all of this? Those are mental games you do not need in your life. Clearly, he has an issue. So no matter how much you are feeling a guy do not go all out for the sake of your feelings. Let him match what he is asking of you. Don't be another random girl in his contact list. Some men like for you to reciprocate everything they do. Some guys do not mind taking the lead in the courtship or relationship. Go with the one who will take the lead in the courtship. It is time out for the guys who only want to toy with your emotions. One day you two have a bond, the next day you two are dating, the next day the two of you are in a relationship, the next minute you were nothing at all. One day you are his woman then after that, he says you two are just kicking it. Please get off of that emotional rollercoaster. God is not the Author of Confusion.

MEN AND THEIR BEST FRIENDS

Not in all Situations but you have to make sure the girl that is his real close friend or real close homegirl isn't where his heart is at. Some male and females can truly have an honest, pure friendship no feelings there just Homeboy, Homegirl. In some cases when all he talks about is his home girl, His Sis it could or couldn't be an issue for you. Some of those friendships are two friends who have feelings for each other, but it would be too complicated to be together.

So there is a mutual understanding that hey we are friends. I may be in love with you but you know we can't be together. When you're in a relationship with a man, and there's this one person he is particularly anal about keep an eye on that situation. Like no matter how much you trip about her she is still there and is going to be there. He will give you your walking papers before he cuts her out of his life. That could end up being a major problem. As a woman, if you know that you have an indecent friendship with a man that is in a relationship. Don't play that woman like she is crazy or jealous of you when deep inside you know, and he knows the friendship the two of you have is inappropriate or maybe was at some point. Respect his relationship. Don't play innocent when you know what his woman is feeling is right and that she is not tripping for anything. Don't be like that because your turn will eventually come. Make it Right.

MEN ARE EMOTIONAL BEINGS

Men are bipolar too. They talk about women being so emotional and moody. One moment they want a relationship one day they want to be married the next day they don't know anymore. You just make sure that your heart stays stable while they go through the whirlwind of emotions. I believe their fear runs deeper than ours when it comes to love. You sometimes have to walk on eggshells when it comes to them because you will be wondering what happened what did you do for him to pull away but it is nothing that you did. The level of their fear causes them to look for any reason not to go through with it. Be strong enough to handle his emotions without getting in yours. When you get to the point where you have to start asking questions like is he still interested what are we doing am I bothering you, you have to ask yourself are we headed in the right direction? Guys will do everything they can to make you fall in love, but the moment you do they scream, they don't want a relationship. Now you're stuck in love right, where he wanted you. In that place where you can't move on because you're in love. He knows that and takes advantage of it.

UNNECESSARY LIES

If he is lying to you then no matter how much you progress, you are going nowhere. You cannot build off of a lie. You cannot build off of lies. Some people feel that small lies are nothing major. Well if that was the case if he lies about little things you don't stand a chance when it comes to major issues. Unnecessary lies are the ones I hate. The lies where the two of you are not even in a relationship, but he is telling you lies. Lying about where he is at, lying about his relationship status, lying about his age just random unnecessary lies. I have had guy's back to back lie about their age. Lie about their name.

Lie about not having kids. Lie about being saved. I am still shaking my head. If I just meet you and already in the getting to know you process, you start telling lies that is my sign to lie myself right on out of that situation. I'm just kidding but pay attention to those types of things. Don't take them lightly. Don't laugh it off. If you hide your real name from me; I have to ask myself what are you hiding from me. Who are you really? I'm not talking about being catfished online. I'm talking about real life meet someone, and they give you a fake name, fake age, fake life. Maybe they didn't expect you to be around long enough to find out the truth. I will never know. You may never know. I do know that it is hard to trust someone who starts off telling full blown lies. If they are hiding their identity, they'll hide you.

They can be living a whole other life without you knowing because they have sold you sweet nothings and half-truths in the beginning. Do not let these guys set you up for failure. Pray for me because I like to verify everything. How old are you again? Is Ronnie your real name, like is that your Birth name. Do you mind if see your Driver License Please? Some guys may think you are crazy and overboard, but to the pretenders, they will be in for a rude awakening. You cannot just take them at their word that prevents them from having to prove themselves to be trustworthy. I do not care how over the top you may feel, or some may think you are but take care of yourself.

THERE ARE MEN GOLD DIGGERS OUT THERE

You have to let some people know you have gotten off that you were going to get from me all the love you got all that you're going to get out of me now, but I'm moving forward. Stop letting men use you for what they think they can get from you. This is not every guy but some guys only talk to women they think have money. They date you with motives; they find out you have good credit, and they think of all the things they can get put in your name. Some of them would even leave the woman who has been down with him from forever because he feels she can no longer benefit him. You have to understand that a man that is ready and prepared for you will not come to you looking for what you can do for him, but he will have the mindset of what he can do for you. He will be willing and ready to provide for you add to you bring security to you in more ways than one. Avoid the gold diggers. Don't be moved by a guy who initially comes trying to spend big money on you, willing to pay for everything, etc., because later he is going to need bigger financial favors from you.

Chapter 6

Standards

DO NOT ALLOW HIM TO BE EMPOWERED BY YOU STAYING

𝓘s crazy how people can leave something they know they love just to take a chance at something they think they want; it shows just how much your desires can be detrimental at times. You have to leave room for a man to do what he is going to do. As much as you want to cling to him some nights you have to say, good night I am going to sleep early. Get off the phone first sometimes. Give him room. They don't like crowded space. They like to be free or at least feel that they have freedom. As women, we want to give all types of clues of what to do and not to do, but sometimes you have to let him walk on his own, stop holding his hands. Yes, there is a point where you communicate and let him know what you expect from him, but even after that you still have to step back and see what decisions he will make on his own without you leading and guiding him to make right choices. You'll never know the type of man you are dealing with unless you just give him the room so you can see who he is for real.

YOU MUST REALIZE THAT YOU ARE GOOD ENOUGH

Genesis 1:31

And God saw everything that he had made, and, behold, it was very good

How do you expect a man to believe that you are a good thing and don't know yourself? You can't fake this to make it. Your confidence in yourself should be evident. Thank God for a man that will come along and encourage you in that, but you should know it yourself. You are good enough to have God's best regardless of your shortcomings, your flaws or anything in your past. You are still good enough for the best. Whatever you feel like you deserve that very thing you will receive. Some people God blesses them in spite of their insecurities others may not be as fortunate. Until you realize you deserve better God may just let you settle. Until you know your worth, you will be forever aiming below your standards in relationships. Don't accept any man that is presented to you until you understand your worth.

There was a quote I seen on social media that says "when you settle you upgrade the other person and downgrade yourself." You may never get what you deserve until it registers that you owe it to yourself. God has better than your best waiting for you. Every time I felt that I have seen God's Best He always shows me better. If He says He has nothing but the best for you then, Believe Him. Stop settling for only what you can see.

YOU CANNOT BE AFRAID TO LOSE HIM.

Luke 17:33

Whoever tries to keep their life will lose it, and whoever loses their life will preserve it.

You doing whatever to get him to stick around but if he was the one for you, it doesn't matter what come, what may, he will be there. Don't be afraid to set a standard; set rules for the relationship. You cannot lose what you never had. If that man is for you, he is going to be for you to the end. Stop losing it trying to keep him. By all means be attentive to your man. Be attentive to his needs and being aware of your actions. Do the necessary things to maintain the relationship but never be afraid to lose him. Your Trust has to be in God if He gave the man to you and you to the man He is going to keep it together.

BE A LADY FIRST

1 peter 3:4

Rather, it should be that of your inner self, the unfading beauty of a gentle and quiet spirit, which is of great worth in God's sight.

It's Automatic when you act like a lady, He treats you like a Lady, and he automatically knows how to behave like a man. Don't keep hopping from man to man, saying you are looking for a man that will treat you like a lady. You have first to be a woman. It doesn't matter what lifestyle they live. Men do have Respect for Ladies. I've even seen what most would call thugs or guys who are a little rough around the edges line up when they come in contact with a real lady. It first starts with the respect that you have for yourself. A man will only treat you the way you allow him to. If he is not willing to change then, he will probably go for a woman who will accept him the way he is and deal with him on that level. If you present yourself as a lady, a man will treat you just as you are and nothing different. They will try but do not tolerate being treated less than you deserve. You set the standards for your relationship. You show how you desire to be treated by what you allow.

ARE YOU OKAY BEING HIS SECOND CHOICE

Do you want to be a man's second choice; I don't know how I feel about that? Don't sit around and wait while a guy maxes out all of his options before he finally comes to you. If that is who God chose for you, it shouldn't take him a million women before he gets to you. If he is praying and seeking God, it shouldn't take him that long to discover who you are do not wait on the back burner while he waits to see if something better comes along. If he is still looking then, you are not the one for him. When a person finds the one, they stop looking. If his options are open keep yours open. I do not believe in women sitting around waiting for a guy to date you.

It is evident he has probably placed you in the friend zone for whatever reason but don't be his last option. If nothing else better comes then, he will consider you. You will always have that thought in your head that you were not his first choice and began to wonder if you are what he wanted. I would never want to be someone's last option. Would you want someone who chose you after everything else failed? We are in a different time nowadays; women just want a man it doesn't matter if they are selected last if he chose them second or third. It does not matter to them if they are the main chick, side-chick just as long as you have something you can call a man it's acceptable in today's time. I pray women across the globe will begin to raise their value and know the importance of knowing their worth.

STOP FIGHTING OVER A MAN

One of the top reason women doesn't like each other is a man. I have seen a man tear up friendships, families, and even churches. Women wouldn't be friends with each other because of the possibility of losing an opportunity to be with a guy if they befriended each other. They cannot be friends for the sake of an opportunity to be with a guy they both probably like. I know there is a shortage of men or maybe and overflow of women, but it is not that serious where women can't come together for the sake of a man.

Men stick together all the time. They are going to be friends, homies, and partners forever and they won't think twice of letting a female come in between their friendship. Not women, a woman will cut every girl that comes in a 50 feet radius of the guy she is interested in. As you can see, I said interested in half of the time they are falling out over a guy that neither one of them has dated they both are crushing on a guy that won't chose either one of them to be within the end. Can I have a minute to talk to women in the church Oh my God? Yes, Women in the Church. Every time a decent man of God walks in the church, he automatically has at least 15 women claiming him as their husband. For the regular random guy that comes in, He has at least 5-7 women claiming him. Not to mention the pastor who has half of the congregation believing they are his real wife, ok, I am done. My point is, women, let us come together. God has someone for you trust Him you don't have to hate other women for the sake of getting or keeping a man. Here's a little nugget for you. You don't have to sit in church for years waiting for the one to walk in, I want to be the one to break the news to you Everybody's husband is not going to walk through those Church doors. He may be at the Bank boo; He may own that sub shop you have lunch at every Wednesday. He may be that lawyer walking past you at the court house as you are on your way to pay the speeding ticket you got last month. Don't limit God. Broaden your options.

When you narrow things down to either this or that it can get discouraging especially when neither one is what you want. So, do this, open up your options, and that will give God plenty of room to do something magnificent. Don't get discouraged at what is currently presented to you. There is something better out there waiting for you. There is a time to narrow down your options, and then there is a time to open up your options. Do not limit God to only what you can think of; there are so many ways you can meet him, so many different locations where you can meet him. It can happen at any place or anytime.

SIDE CHICKS ARE SIMPLY A SPARE

Have you ever seen a spare tire? Yes, the little doughnut tire that hides in the back of the trunk and only comes out when the original tire blows out and is no longer operable. Like my mother says all the time, "If You like it, I Love it." Ladies don't be the one to make his relationship better. He uses you to make him happy in his troubled relationship. If he wants to be with you and he truly finds happiness with you then let him make that move. Let him get it right and do things right. Never start a relationship out of order.

If his situation is complicated, tell him to try again when things aren't so complicated. Stop entering these complex situations. If he is serious about you, he would not even approach you knowing his situation is not right. Be careful with that some guys want to confess oh I'm in a messed up situation right now, I'm getting a divorce, or that's just my baby momma we live together in separate rooms until she gets on her feet. Really, okay. Let us cut this whole side chick thing out. We have to have some morals and let a man know. If you are in a situation, period point blank, we do not have anything to discuss on a personal level.

If he is still in a situation and still bold enough to make an approach with you then what different shall women expect from him? When things get shaky with you, what do you think he is going to do? Don't forget the same way he was just approaching you he did the same thing to the woman he is currently seeing. She once caught his attention just as you did. A Side-chick should be something that is non-negotiable but instead, it is very acceptable, and women hold such pride knowing that you are this man's side piece. I know some things just end up happening that way but don't stay there. If a man loved you, he would be with only you. If he loved one, he wouldn't be cheating with another and if he loved another, did he really love the other. Do not be a side chick be his woman or nothing at all. Do not be an option; any man that will compare you with another woman has got to be out of their mind because truly you are one of a kind. Don't be devalued or feel like you have to allow him to weigh his options. No, ma'am, there is a man out there who knows specifically what he is looking for and who he is looking for and that will be you and only you.

NO STANDARDS

Women don't want to have standards because they know there are not many men who will come up to it. You get rid of the rules and try to do whatever it takes to keep the man happy. You give him whatever he wants and even go over and beyond doing things you think will make him happy. Who need standards when you have the opportunity at having a man in your life? Anything goes right? I do not even want to know what all women agree to just to be in a relationship. We have Swingers in the world, open marriages, polygamy all these different types of agreements. We're in a time where regular sex doesn't satisfy anymore. For sex to be pleasurable. People are urinating on each other, slapping, punching, choking. Whatever you feel is necessary to keep your marriage; just to feel pleasure. Bring God into your marriage, and He will enter your bedroom. Marriage has different meanings to everyone.

To you, it could mean a commitment to one man and one man committing to you for the rest of your life. To some people, marriage is marrying a man understanding that he is your husband and you are his wife, but you open your bedroom to outsiders. Don't be quick to get jealous or want what someone else has because you do not know what they have agreed upon to have that marriage or get that man to marry them. People are doing what makes them happy even if they had to get rid of their morals and standards to have it. Wait for the real thing. It may seem so far away and hard to come by, but it will come, and you won't have to compromise your morals nor your standards.

YOU WON'T ADMIT THIS

You've been through so much you are the point now to where you have even contemplated going to the other side, yeah, dating women. You have almost given up on men. You are looking for a way out of your pain. Maybe a woman will treat you the way you feel you deserve. You heard they know a woman better than a man so you feel they will meet all of you emotional and sexual needs but can I tell you something. The same thing you are running from in men, you will end up finding a woman. If you decided, you wanted to become a lesbian.

Do you know there are abusive lesbians, crazy lesbians, cheating lesbians, controlling lesbians, lesbians that play the same games that men play? So, that won't save you from being hurt. Saying you want to be with the same sex won't stop the pain. It won't be until you get a grip on what you deserve and begin to know your worth pain will forever find you. There is a strong, loving man waiting to love you. He is waiting to minister to your vulnerabilities, to rub your feet, to get your hair done. One who is ready to send you to the spa, waiting to feed you grapes, waiting to make you hot tea, waiting to give you a heating pad and rub your tummy when you are on your menstrual. Yes, he wants to give you all of that and some.

Chapter 7

Wait

IT IS SO EASY TO QUIT

Galatians 6:9

And let us not be weary in well doing: for in due season we shall reap if we faint not.

It is easy to quit, but there's something inside of me that wants to see what will happen if I keep pressing! I have to see what's on the other side of this! I am super excited!!!! It's going to happen for me, and it's going to happen for you, Keep On Pressing. Do not give up in the process. Everything will turn out well for you in spite of all of the mistakes, bad decisions they will be turning into blessings for you. I do not care how many wrong relationships, how many break-ups, you are going to end up with the right one if you do not quit. You have to keep going. Just know that you are at the Edge of your Breakthrough. Don't give up right before it happens.

GIVING YOU THE BEST

Proverbs 27:17

As iron sharpens iron, so one person sharpens another.

God will prepare you for the Worst and then Give You the Best. You can go through so many wrong relationships but if you didn't go through them would you have an appreciation for a good one? Don't take a good relationship for granted. You should have a greater appreciation the next time around. Sometimes as women we can be very ungrateful and start to nag about the little things. There's nothing wrong with making things better in the relationship you should be able to make each other better. I would rather have a relationship where we are working on a few minor things rather than the relationship where you are trying to find something good in it and the guy. When we go through the worst, we can't help but appreciate the Best when it comes. Get ready for it!

HIS LOST HER GAIN

Philippians 3:7

But whatever were gains to me I now consider loss for the sake of Christ.

Never feel that you lost your whole world when a man walks out of your life. If he walked out, it is evident to you his decision as well as yours. Do not lose yourself. It will never be your lost it will be your gain. God will never allow you to lose in a situation where you have given your all to someone it is his lost, not yours. God always have a ram in the bush. Not to say hop out of one situation and go into another one. Just know that that one was not the one. I have this saying if something is for you, you never have to stay stuck or go looking in your past for it. If it's meant to be, you can move forward, and he will come back around. If it is supposed to be, you can't go wrong moving forward; it will come back to you. But never think your whole world is over because someone walks out of it. You will gain more than you believed you have lost.

DON'T LEAVE EMPTY HANDED

Romans 8:28

And we know that in all things God works for the good of those who love him, who have been called according to his purpose.

Just saying if you are going to go through hell, come out with something. You never go through things just to be going through them. There's something in it for you. Don't leave Bitter and Empty

Handed! Whenever you walk out of a relationship, do not leave feeling like you wasted your time and all of your efforts. You do not have to go Empty handed. What did you learn in the Relationship? Whatever mistakes you have made should make you better for the next relationship. Focus more on what you did, what did you get out of it. The more you concentrate on that you will see the strength and wisdom received and those same things can be the very tools you can use to move forward in the next relationship. When you leave feeling like you left with nothing. You will probably end back up in a similar situation until you leave with what God intended for you to get. It is never for nothing.

YOUR TIME LIMIT KILLS YOU

Ecclesiastes 3:1

To everything, there is a season and a time to every purpose under the heaven:

You can't put God on a timer. You set a certain time for things to happen and when it doesn't, it hurts you. God doesn't work by your clock. The wait would not be so bad if you will take off the time limit you have given God. If you have already made your request known to God, then wait for Him to fulfill it. Live your life, and in the meanwhile, He will bring it to pass. It's hurting you because you are breaking your promises and you're breaking your own heart. You said you would be married last year God did not mention that. You cannot get upset when He does not bring to pass the things you want when you want them. He has a set time to bless you. Trust that His timing is perfect. Get caught up in God. Get caught up in what you love; the man will find you doing that very thing. Stop with all the crying and all the fasting to get God to move a little quicker. That thing that pleases Him is your Faith. Know that He is going to do it. Know that it will happen. Take the Limits off, and that will give him the Time and Space that He needs to move. Sometimes the wait is about you trying to figure out what you want before God sends it. One minute you want a Thug, A Christian Thug, the next minute you want a white man that works in Corporate America, next time you want a man that's diverse so he can speak to you in His native language. The truth is you do not know what you want or what you need so take the time to figure out who you are, so you can choose to be Chosen by the Right mate.

PREMATURE BLESSINGS

Birthing things out season can be bittersweet why because you have what you want but the struggle is real. What do I mean the struggle is real? The blessing wasn't prepared, it was not ripe, it was not matured, and it was not ready. Have you ever picked a fruit off of a tree, let's say for instance you look on a plum or apricot tree and you pick out the biggest juiciest green plum you can find, and although it looked very green and seemed to be filled with sweet juice, you wash it, rinse it, just to taste it and see that it wasn't ripe. It was sweet to have but bitter to taste. Bigger isn't always better. Before you get yourself into a situation with someone, make sure the timing is right for it. He may seem ready, acting grown, talking grown but what will you find inside. You wanted it so bad; you just couldn't wait. If God gave you a word, a promise and you go out and make that thing happen. Yes, you may still get it but are you going to be able to cultivate it, nurture it to the state God intended it to come. When a woman has a premature baby, she can't just take the baby home. Although it came early, the baby still has some developing to do, so they may put the child in an incubator to secure the complete development of the child. It was not carried out the full term. Some of us have entered too many preemie relationships, preemie marriages, and underdeveloped blessings. If they are not careful with the preborn child, they are still at risk of losing the child. The same thing when you birth premature things, it may look developed on the outside, but there is still that risk of something happening in the developing process on the inside. Premature blessings are in a critical state; they need extra care and extra caution. So take precaution when you are rushing God's hands to get the blessing to you. Let it completely develop so that you may enjoy without all the risk, and precaution you can just enjoy what the Lord has done.

YOU DESERVE THE RING

Understand that you are Worth the Ring. You are worth the Wait. Stop letting the men with bad or good intentions swindle you into giving them what they want without giving you a ring. You are worth it. Why wait and just let a random guy come along and get what belongs to your husband? You are not that impatient; you can wait. Whether you give it up or not the wrong one will leave, regardless. Why keep risking it, though? Marriage isn't that far away. Save yourself for the right one. It is crazy how we cherish material things more than our sacred things. We won't even lend our car to someone because you don't want them to wreck it or drive it all crazy. If you do find someone who you trust to drive your car what do you do? Give a background check do you have a driver license, are they valid? You give instructions; you can use my car but don't drive out all of my gas, don't bring it back empty. Do not speed in my car, be careful don't wreck my car, be careful don't be hitting the potholes in the street. You give instructions. Why then do you just put your heart in every hand that smiles at you? Does he have a license? Will he leave your heart on empty? Will he take your heart down and bumpy road and hit every pothole he could find? Stop handing over the keys to your heart to every man that you meet.

HOW CAN I TELL IF I'M RUSHING?

Raise your hand if you are a woman who has bought your own wedding ring! Yes, women buy their wedding rings. That could be a sign that you are rushing. I am not condemning or bashing women that have bought their own ring. I encourage you to let that man work for you. Let him work to get you your ring. You deserve a proper proposal. It is true every situation will not be the same. Some of you will get married in some of the strangest ways. Some will have court house weddings, some will elope, and some will have fairy tale weddings. Whichever one you may have make sure it is of God. You will know if it is of God. All of the questions in your head that man should answer not with his mouth but with his actions. If you are pushing for marriage, you will find yourself doing things like buying your ring. He should be initiating marriage, not you. You shouldn't be dropping hints and clues every chance you get. It is ok to let him know that marriage is your goal from the beginning. He does not need a daily reminder. Also, ladies do not let a man rush you into marriage either. Some guys will force you or be a little pushy about marriage. For the most part that is good but be careful. You do not want to get caught up in a marriage that was not ordained by God. When you rush, you will know by the things you are doing out of order and by the things you are doing before time. You also have to know no matter how much you push or pull, If a man doesn't see you as his wife, he will never see you as his wife catch that. You can cook clean hand wash and press his clothes. All he will see is a girl who has done all of these extra things that he does not deserve, trust me he knows when he doesn't deserve it. It doesn't necessarily make his eyes open to you being his wife. When his eyes are open, you wouldn't have to bend over backward to get him to see you are a wife or you're his wife.

GOD WILL SHOW YOU THE TRUTH

When you want to know the truth God will show you. If I was dealing with someone who had a woman or girlfriend, he was lying to me and lying about her. Even if a man denies another woman just to be with you, it is still your responsibility. You can't say well I will take his word for it but deep inside you know ten times out of ten he is still dealing with a person still dating her, still in a relationship with her, still having sex with her. There are women out there who are just pure out crazy and refuse to move on and let a man go but for the most part if you catch a woman tripping out over a man. He is being untruthful with you and is telling her lies as well. Women act crazy for a reason. If you're a woman, you must know women don't act crazy with a man for no reason at all. Most women do deal with jealousy, but that doesn't mean that every woman is jealous and they just won't move on. Guys can be slick. They will tell this woman they don't want the other woman; she just won't leave him alone; you're not smart if you believe that. Now you think that he just has this crazy derange ex-girlfriend that won't go away and you want her to let you enjoy your relationship with him.

A guy may be done with a female but if he doesn't properly end the relationship with the old woman and just try to move on to the next one. There's going to be some issues. I believe that is the problem with most of these situations. The way some guys try to just play one female for the next. Women don't like being played. We are strong beings we can handle the truth but cannot swallow a lie. We hate being lied to but be honest tell the woman the truth. Of course, she will snap and probably go crazy for the next 2-3 days, but she can't be mad and hold a grudge towards you when you have told her the truth Tell a woman a lie, and you just might have to deal with her for the rest of her life. You will get the drama when you treat a woman cold. Even if a man does not give you the closure, you need ladies you still have to be strong enough to still find closure within yourself.

BE PATIENT WAIT ON GOD

There is someone He has specifically designed to walk with you. What you desire is out there, you just have to learn to wait for it. Be patient knowing that it will come to you. I pray that you will find True love, something that will not be temporal but last forever. If you know, a person is not for you don't be afraid to let it go. I am not saying it will always feel good but just know that it must happen for you to receive what God has for you.

Chapter 8

Live

KEEP YOUR LIFE

Don't put your life on hold to become everything that he wants and need. It is important for you to maintain your life. Keep your boot camp workouts on the weekend. If on Monday nights you have coffee and read books with Mandy faithfully keep doing so. No man wants to come home to a woman who has been home all day doing nothing but trying to figure out where he has been, why you haven't called, you didn't respond to my text. If you had a life, you wouldn't have the time to think of all that nonsense. Keeping your life is important. If things grow and mature into something major, then you begin to alter things that will work for the two of you. If Monday nights turn into movie night with your man, then do that but never stop living and breathe solely upon the life that the man has; now you want to go everywhere he goes.

Pool night with the boys you want to be there, a game night you are there, fishing trip you are there. Can the man breathe? Try scheduling things with the girls while he is out then you will have him wondering what you are doing, and you're wondering what he's doing, now when you guys come together, there is an opportunity for conversation and even a chance for him to miss you. Guys need space. End of the day. You do too for the sake of you not smothering him and your piece of mind.

REMAIN DESIRABLE.

Don't let yourself go. Stay up to date. Like Beyoncé said in Cater to you, I keep my Hair Fixed, Rocking the hottest outfits. Keep his attention not by being seductive but by staying attractive. Deal with your Insecurities. You have to rid yourself of fear and rejection. You will not be able to tell when you are single. You won't know until you are healed from previous relationships until you are in another relationship.

Well dating again. Never get comfortable in your relationship. When to become comfortable in a relationship? NEVER. You will always have to keep it up tend to your relationships you can't afford for any negative seeds to take root and grow in between your relationships. You do not need Jasmine with the good hair to slide in on the areas where you are lacking.

When another woman wants your man, she plays off of your shortcomings, your flaws or in any area that you are slacking. So, if you wear a ponytail, jeans and tee shirts all day every day then Jasmine slides in with new hair styles every other week.

Her face is Beat, meaning her makeup done very well, every morning before 8:00 a.m. then she uses that to make him feel that he is missing out on something. In reality, she doesn't have the Entire package that you have, but she sure looks like it. So remain desirable. I know you will not be able to be a Beauty Queen every day but do keep yourself up. Dress up for him, don't let yourself go. It's the small things and details that the enemy uses to deceive. Stay on top of that. Do not be walking around with chipped toenail polish, keep your toenails polished, men love cute feet. Smile.

BE STRONG ENOUGH TO NEED A MAN

I want to be your Superwoman, but I would be lying if I said I didn't need a Superman. You can do everything for yourself. You could move the furniture, buy you a house, get you a car, fix your car, buy your clothes, raise your kids, etc. well if you got it all together why will God send you a man? What will he have to do? I know you are strong enough to get things done on your own but know how to step down for the man God sends to take his rightful place in your

Life. If you feel, you don't need a man. Maybe you don't, and maybe you won't get one. Right Men Love to be in control they are not okay with their woman doing everything. So, if you are not ready to step down, you may want to reconsider relationships and marriage because God doesn't need for the two of you to be constantly battling for control in the relationship. That is a major turn off for men. He wants a woman; He does not want to be fighting with his wife over who is the Boss. Let that man be the King of your Castle.

TOO AVAILABLE

Tell yourself this; I'm not too available I made myself too available to you. Never make yourself too available for a man. Even though you have a life, he thinks you have nothing going for yourself because every time he calls you answer. Anytime he needs you; you are there. There is nothing wrong with that but balance it especially if you two are only at the stage of dating or getting to know each other. Make yourself readily available to your mate but not to someone you barely know. Do not play games but do balance the availability you give to him. Instead of always saying yes, say, oh, no I can't today. I am a little busy maybe next weekend. Just balance it do not always throw everything to the curb just because the person calls and wants to do this or that. Think about this most of the time he is calling when he has availability. If you called him randomly all the time and said hey, let us go out, I want to see you today you would probably be somewhere in your feelings because he wouldn't always drop everything on the spot to do what you want when he wants it. The same thing should go for you do not always be available.

BE ALERT AND FOCUS

You have to leave room for a man to do what he is going to do. As much as you want to cling to him some nights you have to say, good night, I'm going to sleep early. Get off the phone first, sometimes. Give him room. They don't like crowded space. They like to be free or at least feel that they have freedom. Keep a Good Balance. No matter how much you are feeling them. No matter how much like them. Be in Control. Do not lose yourself. Don't get caught up. Don't close your eyes and fall in love.

To know what you are getting yourself into keep your eyes open. Stay centered. Stay calm. Get to know him. Let the connection be genuine. Let things Flow. Let the vibe be genuine. You may not end up entering a relationship or getting married guess what, you will end up with a friend. No hard feelings. Things turn out so much better when you do not force it into something God never intended it to be.

Chapter 9 Dating

What do you consider a Relationship?

Find out what is his idea of a relationship you will be amazed at what people call relationships these days just ask to be sure you both are on the same page. When I think of a relationship, I think of quality time. I think of making plans, getting know each other but what is he thinking maybe a sexual relationship? Worldly men are not the only ones who try to enter sexual relationships there are people in the church who believe it's ok to do that, back to the point they may be thinking something entirely different. If he is not ready to settle down, don't worry there's somebody out there who is willing.

You deserve better than chasing someone while he runs the streets. Make sure you have an understanding of what a relationship is to him because we have it mapped out one way in our head but to them, it is something entirely different. He may be sincere about his relationship with you. He may have intentions of treating you like a lady, taking you out and all of the things that a guy does to make a woman feel special at the same time he could think that it is ok to have a female on the side just for extra sex. He actually may believe there is nothing wrong with that as long as he is making sure you are happy and all of your needs are satisfied. So you have to ask, what type of relationship are you looking for? Committed? Open? We are in a different time we are living in you have to ask just to make sure you both are talking about the same thing. People have differences of opinion on what is considered a relationship. We all think different. Your idea of a relationship may not be the same as theirs, discussed that in the beginning stages of your courtship.

YOU WANT IT, BUT HE HAS TO WANT IT TOO.

If you walk up and hand somebody, a Diamond not everyone would take it why because who would think that it is real? Diamonds are expensive and pricey, who just walks up and gives away a diamond? So, of course, someone would reject it because there has to be a defect somewhere or they would think that it is not real.

That's how guys feel when you give yourself up too soon. It's unbelievable even though it could be absolutely nothing wrong with you, it's just that people appreciate what they pay the price for so it doesn't matter if you were a Cubic zirconia or a real Diamond He paid nothing for you thus far having no value. The point is even though you are feeling a guy you still have to make him pay the price. Let him understand your value let him see how much you are worth. His efforts show how much he is willing to pay for you.

IT'S NOT YOU IT'S HIM FOR REAL

Your mind wants you to think something is wrong with you but it's not there's something wrong with him. So if a guy says it's not you, it's him just take his word for it. If he is not ready, let him go on and leave even if you are a good girl someone who is good for him and to him. You may be exactly what he wants, but at the time he does not want to go through the process of lying to you, hiding his ways from you. He knows he is not ready. As much as he may want you, he knows his flesh is getting the best of him. Do not take that to heart. Women always say you would rather the man tell you the truth than lying to you. So when he says he is not ready, believe him. It isn't you, it is him.

GET TO KNOW THE MAN

Get to know your partner, the person you are dating. It will lead to a better connection, better communication, and fewer arguments. Yes, arguments do happen in the process of getting to know someone. Why, because of failure of getting to know that person. If you fail to get to know each other, there will be a misjudgment, no understanding which will kill the relationship. Don't jump the gun because of attraction and chemistry take the necessary time to be sure of compatibility; Don't allow the conversation get fleshly too quick if you just met and already talking about sex there's no need to ask if the relationship is of God or the flesh. Every story is different some people have jumped straight into the flesh, and by God's Grace, they are still together, married, etc. However, that may not be what's best for you and your situation. When your relationship is fleshly, you will know. If you happened to crossed that line you would know because you will be arguing, fighting, jealousy creeps in all of that.

The reason I can say that is when someone is getting to know someone there is a boundary there will be an honor, a sign of respect there. What I'm trying to say is keep the respect as long as you can, and it will be a strong foundation for your Marriage. The decision is yours but to have sex before marriage is a risk it may lead to Marriage it may not. Can you handle your emotions if he walks away from you after that and doesn't marry you.

He leaves you with empty feelings. Now you're trying to heal yourself when God just intended for you to get to know the person and if it didn't work you didn't lose anything, and the two of you could bow out gracefully and still be friends. The good part about it is you are still on the market no damages. It didn't work, and you don't have a soul tie to severe. Let's keep it moving.

DINNER QUESTIONNAIRE

If you have determined that you are going out on a date during the conversation the questions should lead to you getting to know things about him that will determine if he is the one for you. I don't understand why some people say personal background questions are to be off limit while on a date. Even at a business meeting or lunch, they learn the core of who you are, are you single, married your interest hobbies. These few background questions can save you a whole lot of heartache, time and pain. You, my friend, have waited too long to deal with a complicated situation. I believe certain things should be off topic during a date like sex topics, what position do you like; when was the last time you had sex are all questions that let you know where you will eventually be headed and that is straight to the bedroom. It is not rocket science sometimes all it takes is for you to watch and listen

CUT TO THE CHASE

Just when you thought things was going well, you notice engraving of a ring print. Yes, a wedding ring. Why Lord? Why, after him passing everything on the checklist, his hair, great teeth, he's toned, he's funny, he's Intelligent, he's creative, he's perfect. Now dinner is over you are in the lala-land land but wait I forgot to ask one thing are you Single? To your surprise, he told you everything but the fact that he's married. Ladies let us cut to the chase. How many times have you felt you met the one he was so perfect, but the only thing wrong was he belonged to someone else? Cut to the chase go ahead and ask about his current relationship status. A man will ask if you are single and you think because he is asking you that it means he is single. That is not true most of the time. They will ask you hoping that you will not ask but I wonder if you ask right away will he tell you the truth. He probably would, but many women never take the time to ask they like to assume. We know what they say when we assume something right? Yes, no need for me to say it.

PURPOSE OVER EMOTION

You have to put your purpose over your emotions you may want this and want that, but you never put it over your purpose. That is called using wisdom. Make sure the person you are going to spend your life with has a purpose that is compatible with yours. I am not going to say you two should have the same goal because sometimes two people called to do the same thing can pull them in separate directions. Sometimes the differences come together very well. You may love Ryan, praying that God will deliver him, set him free and let him be that rough around the Edges Thug man of God that you have always wanted, but it doesn't always work like that. Ryan has to want God and be willing to give up some things to walk with you. This man has to fit the purpose God has called you to. You can't be worrying about your man's location and trying to do what God called you to do at the same time. You do not need that type of stress in your life. How to handle options? When you're an attractive woman as a woman period, all kinds of people are going to come to you, but you have to choose the one that is best for you, ask God to make it clear to you that He is the one read the story of Isaac and Rebekah. God will give you a better selection to choose from once you eliminate all the wrong ones. Purpose over emotions ladies.

COMPROMISING YOUR DREAM MAN

Do not Compromise. It's not something that you should have to think about but what do you do at that moment where you have dated this guy, that man, that friend and it's the same old same old. Is there always going to be a level of compromise? If you date this man, then you are going to have to deal with this or deal with that. This guy is hard working, but he's very insecure, controlling and jealous. This guy is saved, so he says. He is in church faithfully, hands raised, speaking in tongues, the tears, don't mind worshipping, he'll lead your hand in prayer. But he's still smoking, naked pictures in his phones and says that he just have not had the time to delete them out of his cell wait I'm confused, but you use your phone all day all day. Then you have the brother who is intimidated by your leadership abilities he wants to lead but not following Christ himself. He wants you to submit to him, but he submits to nothing or no one. So, you have to go throughout the entire relationship, explaining yourself, Oh, I didn't mean it like that, because he's dealing with offense. So, he always tears you down, so that he may feel bigger. You can't be yourself because it is offending him. You cannot walk in who you are as a woman of God, to them you are trying to act spiritual and think that you're better than them. A Man that is jealous of his woman is one of the biggest turn-offs, I've ever seen in my life.

I know you're tired of settling for the least and not reaching for what you deserve. You do deserve a man that only wants you. You do deserve a man who will be faithful to you aman that will provide and protect you. A man that will love everything about you and everything that concerns you. A man who will not be intimidated by your strengths. Isn't it funny how you accept their struggles and even things they just do out of habit, but you have to be the one that changes to make the relationship work? They won't accept your insecurities; they won't deal with your emotions, but you have to deal with them just the way they are or else.

It is so easy to find someone you want but to locate the one that is meant is a different story. I'm pretty sure, if you wanted to be married right now, you have a few men hanging around right now ready to buy you a ring and get you down that aisle, but you are still choosing to wait. You want to wait for who God has for you. Sometimes you think maybe you've missed it but listen God won't let you miss what he has for you. I don't care how many of your Ex's are getting married after your break up or how many guys who were trying to talk to you and got married after you turned him down gently, you didn't miss the mark. I hope you are happy for them because yours is coming. Keep being steadfast. Don't be moved. Trust God.

DATE ACCOUNTABILITY

Please have some form of accountability never go off anywhere with any guy alone. Especially without anyone knowing where you are. If you go out on a date with a guy you just recently met, you don't have any business going back to his place or a room with them. I wonder how many women in the world are missing right now without a trace because they went out with a random guy and no one had a clue of who she was with or who the guy was; she didn't even know him. Now she is missing without a trace. I encourage women to leave a trail. If you want to take me out, I need a picture of your identification. I need to know where we are going. Yes, I need to know that and before you get in the vehicle with him sneak and take a picture of his tag number and send it to your date accountability partner. Yes, I am overboard. You should be too. Always be safe. I don't recommend hopping in a car with a guy you just met. You cannot pick me up from my house. I do not let men know where I stay. I don't know you. You should not have my personal address. Particularly, as a single woman who lives alone. Meet him in a well-lit public location, where some security cameras are around. Turn your GPS location on so your phone can be tracked. I know, I am too cautious, right? Nope, I am not. I am protecting myself. I want you to protect yourself. Find someone who you can trust with that information. Don't ever put yourself in a messed up situation. It may never be the case, but I am telling you to use wisdom.

SINGLE PARENTING DATING.

You have to understand that your child or children may or may not be completely comfortable with you and the dating scene. Every man should not meet your child. Especially not right away. If I have introduced anyone to my daughter, they were called mommy's friend. You don't want to confuse your child. Focus on dating someone you know is worth the try. Everyone you have dated was not worth it. You already knew they weren't the one you just wanted someone to date. I don't recommend it, it takes away your energy, and it will eventually leave you emotionally drained even if you feel like you can handle it. You will soon see the ultimate toll it will have on you. Making sure your children are comfortable with who you bring around is vital. Women I cannot express the importance of being careful what man you are bringing around your children.

I know some of you do not see anything wrong with dating younger men be careful with how young you are going. It is just awkward having someone around your daughter who is not far from her age. As grown as he may be acting he is still young and don't be surprised if he is still attracted to more adolescent girls this is not every case. Not just with younger men but older men too. You need to know the history of their family, find out if they have been sexually abused or if sexually abuse has happened in their family. There are ways to find this out without asking hey do you like little girls. Don't offend anyone.

Have a talk with them. I do it. I do not care who they are or how old they are; I will ask them can I trust you enough to bring you around my child? It is important to me that the man I am with can be trusted with my kid whether I'm around or not. Will you see her as your child? How will you look at her or him? Remember your mate has to be a perfect match for you and your children. You have to be careful. Some guys will come to you and even marry you just to get close enough to prey on your child. You do not know what internal issues they are dealing with; stop falling in love because of looks and sex. There are too many stories that are out there concerning these matters. Choose Wisely.

You have that responsibility of protecting your children. I'm discussing this because I have come across many stories where mothers ignored the fact that their child was being molested or raped but because the mother wanted the man around they ignored their child's confession; they ignored what they knew was true just to keep the man. They accused their child of lying because they didn't want to acknowledge the fact. Do not let that be you. You can tell. You can see. You can pick up on vibes. Trust them. If you cannot trust him with your children, you do not need to be with him.

SINGLE MOTHER'S

I really want to encourage the single mothers, listen you are just as Good as any other woman. I know what it is like to be picked over because you have a child. The thing about it is, I would not want to be with anyone who would not accept my child. My daughter and I are both a Good thing. There are guys I wouldn't consider marrying because even though they were perfect me, they were not a good match for my daughter. The same thing for you as a single mother the man you marry, date or be with has to be a good match as far as a husband and a father. Whether the child's father is active in the child's life or not the man you are with will be the father figure in the household. He has to embrace your child. Any man that looks you over because you have a child or children does not deserve to have you. Keep waiting it takes a Godly man to come in and get the job done. Don't be discouraged I don't care if you have twelve Children if he wants you he wouldn't care, and he would do what is necessary to get the job done. Any man that will see a woman shortcoming, and run because he does not want to do anything about it I'm not sure how I would look at them. A lot of guys would run, but that is good because it leaves room for the special God sent guys to come in and do what God sent them to do, and that is to love you and your children.

Chapter 10

Healing and Growth

TRUE HEALING

Real Healing is being able to walk in love in spite of being hurt by a person or situation and being able to love still. A lot of people feel that because they have physically said out of their mouth forgive me because they have hugged or given a handshake to that person that they forgive that person. The problem here is forgiveness is an inward thing. If you are an individual who has outwardly demonstrated a form of forgiveness, you should know that forgiveness starts from inside to outside. To be able to drop on your knees and say, Lord Jesus, I am bitter; I hate this person. I hope she won't make it I hope he won't make it. They should have never hurt me. How can I let that go? They deserve to go through something look at what they put me through. So now you are jealous because they seem happy and left you hurt and wounded. Now your anger has kindled, and now you want to call and make the person frustrated you want them to be miserable for what they did to you. Now you want to become a living hassle to them especially if you had a child by them. You see them, and they're with that other brother or sister and spending the money that they never had when they were with you. Now they are doing all the things to him or her that you argued and fussed about the entire relationship. Now you want child support, or you want to drop the kids off to let him know that he still have to deal with you.

Poor children caught in the middle of this thing. Now, if you're the man, and you left one woman, but now she is out looking better now dressing like nobody's business, wearing things that she would never wear for you. Her hair is done, nails are done, and she has a smile on her face. When you left her, she walked around the house in bleached shorts, a ripped shirt, faded sweat pants with a scarf around her head. Now she is dressing up for this new guy. She is cooking him meals that you could not get if your life depended on it. Give yourself a hand clap you did a marvelous job in helping mold that woman or man. I know you are still mad about it but let it go. Don't be moved by what you see because he or she will go through a perfecting with that next brother or sister. So don't hate congratulate.

You are looking at how they improved after they encountered you. Look at yourself they got better, and you got bitter. They are glad they moved on because you are still the same angry person you were when they were with you. Be better and be better for real do not pretend to be doing better just to convince them.

LOOK FOR YOUR GROWTH.

Look for how you have become better. One thing we begin to do is look for a reason of why. What if there is no reason why. What if God never gives you a reason of why it did not work? That can be one of the worst types of hurt the ones without cause. Jesus did nothing wrong to Judas, yet Judas own issues were the problem. Why someone hurt you may never be explained just know that God is working it for your good. It is not as bad when you see someone wrong you, hurt you, leave you, betray you, steal from you, and you see them punished for it, or you see them reap what they have sown.

My question is what if they never reap what you feel they should. What if they never pay for what they did to you. I have been there. I wanted that man to hurt. I wanted him to pay for everything he ever did to me. I wanted him to pay for it. He deserved it. He deserves to suffer for what he did for me. Why shouldn't he suffer if I had to? Why shouldn't that sister pay for what she did to you? When she gets a man in her life, you never approach her but you out of spite flirt with her man to give her a taste of her own medicine. What an evil game to play. Grow from your pain; don't let it stunt your Growth.

REJECTION

Rejection is painful. It messes with your self-esteem and your self-worth. It causes you to feel inadequate. In the area that caused it and it trickles down into other areas of your life. Perfect Love cast out all fear. It is okay to be rejected but it doesn't feel good. Rejection has nothing to do with your self-worth. It has nothing to do with your value. Think about how many people reject God, and He is the one who breathes life into them daily. Even God goes through rejection. Jesus went through rejection it didn't change the fact of who He was people just chose not to receive Him, and people will decide not to accept you. Don't let that break you or bring you down.

WOMAN BE WHOLE
POETRY

The Birth of Me

I have been in Travail for some time now, wondering when will I see the birth of what I have been carrying. At times I have been discouraged, feeling barren, but I came to a place of realizing that what I was carrying all along was me. That heavy burden, the pain, and all of the heartaches was for me to become the Woman of God I am today. I have looked at everyone's life and compared it to mine. Questioning God, about where's my manifestation. I was looking for something tangible, something I can touch, something I could see with the natural eye. I had to get to the place where I stopped looking for a material birthing; it was a Spiritual Birthing. I had to stop looking at the Blessings of everyone else's life and look at what the Lord had done for me. The moment I changed my perspective was the moment I saw the New Me, The Better Me, The Stronger Me, The Wiser Me, The Matured me. I now look back on my life and ask why me, why the turmoil, why so many storms, why so many trials, why so much suffering, Why so much pain, and the answer is because I was in travail giving Birth to the woman God has called me to be. Everything I have ever been through in life was and has been the Birth of Me.

Wondering If what I feel is real

I am wondering how long will you stay. Wondering if you're the type to play with my heart that is, its fear I feel wondering if what we have is real will I believe enough to let down the shield, give us time to build this bond that is…giving me a warmth inside that melts through my bright eyes and glorious smile, wondering if this is worth the while, something I've dreamed of since a child, True love that is…that has me hoping and dreaming again.. just so shocked that something that feels this good but is not sin, just pure pleasure that comes from a deep connection within… wondering will this last or is it something that will pass..trying to move slow making sure this is the right way to go but who knows..these feelings are like the wind that blows..you don't know which direction it flows or from where it came or where it goes.

My Battle with Sin

My heart is heavy with a weight that I can't shake how much more hurt can one woman take. I know it is me. I am the one who keep making the mistake, sinning, and repenting, sinning and repenting. How can you keep forgiving me when I do it over and over again? I keep telling you this is the last time or at least that was the last time. It won't happen again is what I keep telling you. I tell you, I love you, I don't want to hurt you but within that next hour I am doing it again ignoring what I just confessed to you. I want to give my best to you. Don't ever want to risk losing you. I want to draw near to you but what do I do if I can't win because of my lost of giving in to sin, playing with sin. I feel that I'm messing it up and I feel so guilty when I raise my hands to bless you. Knowing that I'm capable of putting them down and going right back to the sin that I was in. I ask myself is it worth it. How many more times will you take me back? How many more times will you comfort me and say that you are with me? I fight against your love, I feel that it's something that I don't deserve. If they only knew my sin I know what they would say because it's what I would say, girl you have some nerve, your worship is not true look at the things you do. If you think that is loving God then you do not have a clue. You are still battling with yourself cannot even embrace the new. Your sin has you stuck like glue but I will snap out of it and say that is not true. I am not my sin yes I struggle but in the end I win. I lift up my hands and confess my sins yes I asked Him to forgive me over and over again. My sin is not where I belong so I will keep fighting it I will never give in to sin. It makes me feel like it is okay but sin is a lie sin is not my friend. It makes me feel that when all else fails that it will be there. When I feel I have no where else to turn sin stands there with open arms to welcome me home. Sin wants to take the place of God. It wants to comfort me when I am alone. It wants to hold me when I am lonely. When everyone turns their back sin makes me feel that it is my homie. Sin you are not my God, sin wants to fill me every time I feel empty sin is a deceiver. It wants the place of God. It wants you to delight yourself in it. It will give you everything your flesh desires. All the while it is putting out your fire. Stealing your zeal infecting your wound so that you will never heal. It wants to kill my passion my dream and to take me outside of God's will. Swants to give you a thrill something tangible that you can feel but when it is over on your table it will place a bill. A bill of what you owe and I want you to know that the price on the bill is your soul.

Proverbs 31: Who Can Find Her

Who can find a virtuous woman a virtuous woman is worth far more than rubies. If you believe that then why are you letting him pull you up to a Ruby Tuesday's. Have you forgotten your worth as a woman? Do not let a man flaunt you around like your some type of ornament because when the season is over decorations get put up in storage like the lion on the wizard of oz where is your courage. Afraid you might miss if you keep your virtue. Do not be like the three bears and let him sample all of your porridge because he is going to go and tell all his boys how he already read that story now instead of a Shekinah Glory you are walking in a faded glory after all the excitement he considers you boring. You did not leave anything to the imagination now he is realizing you was not the real just an imitation of God's true ordination. A virtuous woman is not going to compromise her integrity but she is going to stand firm on God's foundation. She is not going to try and lure you with her body nor a lustful conversation, but she will die to herself turn in prayer and resist temptation. She is not the type to entice you while she skillfully plans her manipulation. She is patient anxious for nothing but everything by prayer and supplication. She is not the type to hold you back because she understands that you are called to reach nations. She is not falling for a man out of desperation because she has compared his love to yours and settling for less she will not even take into consideration. She patiently waits in high expectation of a man that will have a revelation of the two becoming one allowing God to be loved with his most love creation.

About your Hurricane

Have you ever went through the storms of life? Well my storms feel more like Hurricanes, and it came and destroyed so much..you lost the people you loved..you lost everything you worked so hard to get.. the thing you gave all your energy to build up and it was torn down.. everything gone but you. On the other side you turn and look back at everything that was and it hurts because it was a part of you but it was not you. You look down at yourself no scars, no bumps no bruises.. just the dust from the mass destruction, just to let you know where you was.. you can choose to walk around with those same clothes on remembering the horrible experience or you can dust yourself off and look at the damage of your past and say I thank God that was not me.

Because you could have been destroyed in it. We forget that part. Leave your past, it should be destroyed enough that you can't go back that way again. Yes, it is lonely but you are going to new people, places, and things. Receive the Direction that the Lord is leading you quit trying to pick up broken pieces of your past and try making it a part of your future. Leave that mess.. there is more and better waiting for you if you will walk away.

No We Can't Get Married

No we cannot get married if you are not ready to be a husband. Sorry, marriage is more than saying I am yours. There is a role you have to play. A position you have to hold. A child you have to father. A woman you have to mold. It is more than you wanting to be in control fix your plate, wash your clothes. There is so much more to marriage.I am not even moved by the ring no matter the karats. Does your heart belongs to Jesus.. marriage is on your mind but is it for Him or your own selfish reasons. Someone to look good on the side of you; it does not matter how she feels just as long as the happiness looks real. No thanks, I am good. I do not want you to marry me. You will be cheating on yourself, no room for me too much of you. I think we can chill because I do not want to marry you. You have no clue the meaning of marriage to love me like Christ loves the Church. Not give me a bunch of hurts. Christ is second when His place is first what was supposed to be a blessing ended as a curse.

My Love Story

My relationship with Christ it is like I was in the street sleeping around drinking, smoking cussing and fussing and this Godly, Highly anointed, Fine, Handsome, Strong, Wealthy, Educated Brother came up to me while I was in the midst of it and said, I want to marry you and I am like me, nah you do not want to marry nobody like me, Do you not see my lifestyle he was like yeah but I chose you and I love you. So my head is messed up now because who is this man wanting to take my hand in marriage saying that he loves me and he does not know me like that. So I am getting to know him but it seems like we been together for years the Chemistry is mind blowing. So, I marry the Brother, (shoot, I was a sinner but not a fool) I married that man. Things were good for a while; I started going through hard times, arguing at him, because I thought he wasn't going to be there. The storm came and I argued at Him because I did not understand that He would not leave me in the storm. So, now I am in love with Him again. Because He showed me that He is a protector and that He will be with me through it all.. Things was going great again, until my old ways started to creep up again, now I am struggling with being faithful to this man, I am back to sleeping around again, smoking to ease my mind, and drinking to take my mind off of how much, I am screwing up my marriage. So guilt is eating away at me, I am telling myself how much I do not deserve a man like this. He walks in on me and says, Baby why are you beating yourself up, give me this glass, put that out and come here. Now, I am crying because I just know He is going to leave me. Then He pulls me close to him and says, I still choose you and I will always love you. So, I am boo-hooing snot and tears everywhere. He lifts up my head, looked me in the eyes and said. I am not going anywhere. I just fell in His arms and He held me all night long. I woke up the next morning and He brought me breakfast in bed rose petals leading to my Hot Bath and I am feeling all good…like where did this man come from..He had to be sent from heaven, oooou. We have been through so much together and I keep falling in love with Him over and over again. That is the story of me and my husband..Jesus.

What About Me

Lord who looks after me, who cares for me, who checks in on me. I asked over and over again. Where is my help? Where is my shoulder to lean on. Lord where is your hand that uplifts me? Where is your strong arm that rescues me. I pour out of me until there is nothing left then I call on your strength. I ask of this water you have.. may I drink of this water you give. I do not want to thirst again. Lord this time fill me up let the well spring up in me, flow through me. My days of drought are over. No longer will I thirst at this extreme. I must have you. I must. I always want to be others help but you are my help. Where is my support, where is my strength, where is my encouragement pour out your Spirit on me Holy Spirit stand strong in me. I am just asking what about me?

Recovering Love Addict

Love is what you make it. I decided to love you through thick and thin for worse or for better. I said I do before I said I do. At times I really feel like I do not want to love a man again the hurt is so deep. Will I ever be ready to love again? I am so quick to rush into it but my heart is still recovering any little thing feels ten times what it should because of the level of hurt I have been through. I fall in love so easy. So easy to love what do I do. Continue to love God and give no one that place. I will just pass on love, my Lord. Have you ever just felt so much pain that it hurts just to talk about it or you just do not want to spill out the weight of it on anyone else. When all you can do is moan? The weight of pain weighing you down. A pain that causes you to be stuck, stagnant, you are not letting go of the past, you are stuck in the present with a strong hold of the past that will not allow you to move into the future. I have found out that after the press that rope has to break. Loosing you to love freely.

Shedding tears

I love you, from my soul, I long, I yearn for you. I cry out from the depths of my soul. Only you hear my cry, only you hear my heart, screaming Jesus, Lord strengthen my mind, my spirit, my soul. Oh how I need you so desperately, let me not faint in the midst of the race. I am giving it my best shot run with me Lord, defend me, Rescue me. My heart screams Jesus save me from my enemies, save me from me, change my ways, change my heart, change my mind, give me your love that is so patient and kind and Your grace that has forgiven me time after time. These tears I cry fills me inside you will never see them roll down my face because they flow to my most inner place. My tears fill my arms as I lift them to sing psalms. My tears fill my legs giving me strength to press ahead. I cry but there is no one to wipe my eyes. I kick scream and yell but still no one can tell my tears fill my heart to soothe the pain after it's been torn apart.

Waiting on Love

I will obey everything that you say. You are the truth, the life, and the way. For you, I will wait. I will not move I will be still. I am waiting on you. Waiting for you. Patiently I am awaiting. No need to fret. Just relax. You know the plans you have for my life. No need to worry. It is all in your hands. I will not be moved. I will stand. Though I do not understand. I know you are faithful and you remain the same. You sent me love but I must wait until our wedding day. Cannot awake or stir up love, I desire to be kept. So, I must pray for a love that is pure, Holy, no guilt nor shame. Your blessing in marriage I choose to claim showers in abundance let it rain.

Just to be Loved

Just to be loved I poured out my heart my mind, my body, and soul just to be loved. I have tried all types, gangstas, pimps, and thugs trying to find this thing they call love. Growing up it was never demonstrated had no laughs, no kisses, no hugs. Trying everything just to be loved. Lord, it is hard for me to let go off this thing they call love. This condition of my heart wants to keep us apart. Do not let it happen, let nothing separate me from your love. It is you that my soul longs for. I crave you Most High, love me God at a level where I will never want a love that is not yours and not from you. You know the desires of my heart. Align them with your purpose. I love you and my desire is just to be loved.

SHEMEKA MCNAIR

Embrace me

I consecrate myself unto you. I want to express my love to you in so many ways, my Lord, if I had a choice never to do wrong again so that I will never displease you I will make it. Is there a way where I can connect with you and never part. I want to go there with you. Please let me in, embrace me with an everlasting touch from you. Bring me up with you. I choose you. I want to spend eternity with you. Father connect with me in a way no one has seen or heard of before. Can I feel the fullness of who you are? Surround me with your protection, keep harm and danger far from me. Father embrace me, cover me make true love to me. Let us be intimate together. Allow this to be a life-changing experience. This next level in you is of power and of love. Shine bright through me. Make me over. I accept your insight, a new vision and impartation of your Holy purified righteous Anointing.

I'm Your Boaz Ruth

Y ou might as well stay do not even think twice about walking away. I know things might not have gone or went your way. But stand still long enough to hear me say…that everything is alright..it is okay. Just turn your heart back from the place where it went astray. Lifting up your idols before me and showing them off as a display. I do not receive your worship it is not in spirit and not in truth. I am the Boaz that you are referring to Ruth. You are not seeking my kingdom you are trying to find or spend time with your boo. Love is an action word and I sent my Son as proof. If any man would deny himself pick up His own cross and follow me that same way what you are asking for will follow after you. If any man would try and save his own life that very thing He will lose. I come to cut you free from bondage. My child be loose, I have given you authority. So speak to that mountain and say be thou moved. I have given you the choice of life or death which one will you choose?

SHEMEKA MCNAIR

I must worship

I must worship with my whole heart. I must worship in spirit and truth. I must worship the love I need is found in you. I must worship for my heart stands grieved it burns with hurt it is weighed with burdens lost of my loved ones a wise decision caused this division trying to see what is on the other side but disappointment is clogging my vision I must worship. On my knees I pray my vow will awake me in the morning. Spirit of God join me as I long for love within me. I must worship I have been made over but it is not asking much. I am marred in my heart could you touch it up I must worship. As I wait, God minister to me console a broken spirit. Mend this contrite heart. I must worship but I do not know where to start. I must worship my face is drenched with tears from pain bottled up from years yet and still I must worship. Yet I must worship in Spirit and in Truth the love I really long for is found in you.

No more excuses for a man

I am so tired of making excuses for a man not feeling bad anymore for why they do not do what they can. You can not use the fact that there was not a father in place. If there was anything out there you really wanted you would put up a chase. Why can't you connect with me spiritually? But you always want to connect with me physically. No one had to teach you how to lust for me but now you need someone to teach how to have love for me. Please do not give me that just as easy as it was for you to try and feel me up and down it should have been as easy for you to know me in and out. I am not going to raise sand or shout. Just listen closely to what comes from my mouth it flows from my heart, I hope it was from a good start. It does not take a genius to know how to love. Love is a natural instinct that comes from the most inner part of our being. No more excuses for a man.

Lord I Thank you

Lord I thank for saving me. You have called and called for me but my eyes were to blind to see that you were trying to walk me into my destiny. Could this be the beginning of my victory? I am leaving the old me behind it is done it is over it is the past, let us just call it history if it was not for you Lord I would still be crying those tears, those tears of misery, those tears of treachery, allowing all my worries and stressors to place a burden on me. Lord I thank you for carrying me, through all my tough times you were always there you never left my side, silly me still had the nerve to have pride. When you have brought me through some of the toughest things in life. So much pain so much strife. Even through that I will continue to press, continue to strive taking it all in stride, I shall gallantly glide into my success, I shall I arrive. Lord I thank you for loving me, now I have this happiness, this joy, this peace, a feeling that I never knew could be, a vision I could never see, Lord your love is so amazing and so unique, and I just want to thank you for saving me.

Winning the Mind Battle

I am going to win this battle of the mind. I think to the enemy I have been awful kind allowing me to lust for things that I know are not mine. Allowing him to taint my thoughts. Not realizing that it was my soul that he almost bought, taking my eyes off the prize when it is God's face I should have sought, visions and images of the past has been brought. Reminiscing not casting down imagination, not even thinking twice about my salvation. So in a rush some of us cannot wait for the real so we will settle for the imitation. Not listening to the word of God but going with our own dictation allowing our spirits to be subject to assimilation, not with the right but with the wrong conversations, there is only one God but yet we have so many duplications. And we wonder why we go through so many trials and tribulations this is a stage where we should be going through a purification humbling ourselves and proving our dedication, not giving in to temptation. Too much pride to die to ourselves do not want to deal with the humiliation. The time is coming when God is going to bring a separation He is going to know who did and did not seek after Him with desperation. Why do we find ourselves hurt after trying to find a match for ourselves is it because we fail to realize that Jesus is the Greatest collaboration. Instead of being here for man, let Jesus be our motivation. There is no man or woman worth fornication. We should all search our hearts and do a thorough examination before we take our last respiration. We have to win this battle of the mind because we are running out of time. He is warning you now so there will be no more signs. Shutdown the enemies playground and that is when you will find yourself winning the battle of the mind.

Change your Mindset

Our minds have to be open to hear the words that our Lord has spoken. We need to be more cautious of where our attention is focused opening ungodly doors has our spirit man suffocating and choking. And the devil do not care he is laid back with his imps laughing and joking. Because we do not know that behind Godly doors lie a treasure of tokens, so do not think you have it all together walking around all arrogant and boasting not realizing that your flesh is out of control and it is going to have you toasting, better yet like a burnt offering it is going to have you roasting. Why because you are lacking covering do not have any spiritual coating but you are putting on a spiritual front speaking in tongues with your hands raise when in reality you are just showboating, so be honest with yourself are you really living those scriptures that you are quoting. And if you are not living by an example then who are you provoking, somewhere down the line you lost your visions and your hoping's. Do not want to let go of your loving drinking smoking. There is no maturity in that, in fact, your spirit man is still in the park hopscotching and jump roping, in the spirit realm you are lollygagging and slow poking, therefore you cannot contend with the footmen or the horses because of all the baggage that you are toting. I hope you have your pen and pad making noting's because this is not a poem where I just sat back and wrote things. God is using me and it is revelation that I bring. So do you choose to satisfy self or please the king? I know you are looking for your help meet but let the true bridegroom be the first to put on that ring. I know these words may hurt they may even sting, but it is not on my own understanding that I lean, every word ever spoken I really do mean. To the soldiers on the wall ask the father to sharpen your discernment and make it really keen that should not be anything spiritually that goes on unseen. There is no I in team we are all one in unity, some say what I say is critical but I am just edifying everything that I read that was biblical. If you don't understand me he could use the drama to give you a visual, let us quit fighting in the physical and realize that this is spiritual.

Cried out Loud

My eyes have cried all out. Now that my tears are gone. I am going to cry through song, cry through these poems not out of shape fashion or form but out of my pain, out of my storm. I am stepping outside of myself outside of the norm. The enemy is alert I know he is alarmed, he knows I am coming, I am dangerous and armed. Taking back my power and showing him who is in charge. The next time you see me going through pain and in the midst of mourn. Do not give me another tissue, but pen pad or pencil and listen for my coming forth to boom louder than a missile. I do not need a man to spark my light or old flames to be rekindled. I have the fire of the spirit that will speak to you poetic, prophetic lyrics, this is not for everyone, so most will not hear it. The rest intimidated by the Spirit they do not understand the anointing, so they fear it. No one is on the sideline whistling and cheering saying, girl, you can make it. So I try to put on a smile, but the pain still shows I cannot fake it. It is taking everything in me to carry this cross but with the Lord as my strength I know I can make it. I have a destiny to get to a dream to fulfill. I attempted to let it go but it is so embedded in me I cannot shake it, bound in my mind, left the past but my memory kept the traces, Lord take this Egypt mentality and Erase it. Do not want to challenge my oppressor but I have to face it, started out walking ended up running. I am changing lanes switching gears, the Lords providing so I am maintaining, there is no complaining no one can stop or change it. I understand that I'm going through so I can begin my changing. So, when you are done do not just give me a new name, change my language. I am worshipping and praying to you out of my anguish. You said victory is mine and I'm here to claim it my eyes have cried all out, and I have no more tears to spill other than these words you give to express how I feel.

Gift Inside

We have a gift on the inside something the enemy wants to hide. He fights us andattacks us with all sorts of insecurities trying to be sure that it will never rise. Something so powerful he wants to keep us bound and tide. He will have you wondering should I step out or not. Is it the time or is it not the time. Do not allow the enemy to play with your mind. He wants you confused and unable to decide. That way he is allowed to buy more and more time, and in the meanwhile, our brothers and sisters are dying. With murder rape suicide day by day, the rates are multiplying all because the enemies in your car and you are listening to his lying. How do you know what you cannot do if you are not even trying? So what songs have you not yet sang, what dance have you not yet danced, what words have you not yet spoken that will break bondage and cancel every one of his plans I am not trying to be harsh but trying to get you to understand that our Father has given us all a golden chance and all we have to do is step out on faith. God gave you His word so it is guaranteed not to be a mistake. So if you are truly a believer of his word then be sure to abide because in each and every one of us He placed a gift inside.

My Inner Beauty

My inner beauty is far more Beautiful than my outer beauty. So when you search for me do not look at my face and please do not look at my waist. There is no beauty in that, in fact, it is a disgrace. Beauty cannot be defined by looking at my Behind, have you searched for the thoughts that are in my mind. You cannot say you know my kind by reading some zodiac sign. Because my inner beauty is far more beautiful than my outer beauty. I am a virtuous woman so please do not approach me with a what's up cutie, for I am not a chunk of silver but much more like rubies, my father has blessed me with a spirit of knowledge wisdom and understanding, so do not try and get too close thinking that you'll use me. For He has also blessed me with a discerning spirit which gives me eyes to see. So I know what lies behind your smile and grinning teeth. You cannot come to me with just a physical attraction because in the spirit we will never meet. Why because my inner beauty is far more beautiful than my outer beauty.. it is not my body but my Spirit that is as fine as wine. It will be my heart that blows your mind. It will be in the word where we will spend our time. It is not how I walk but who I am walking with that makes me so divine. Like the Father the Son and the Holy Spirit we will be heavenly intertwined, what I do have to offer is not easy to find I am not of this world so this will not be another case of the blind leading the blind. So come with a vision before you final your decision. Because I am a woman of God who He has set out on a mission and I am not letting anything or anyone come and bring a division. So when you look at me Really look at me, because my inner beauty is far more Beautiful than my outer Beauty.

Pleasing in your eyes

Why can't I be pleasing in your eyes? If I did it for them why can't I do it for you? Why can't I be pleasing in your eyes? I did everything in my might to please a man. I thought they were everything I needed; I thought they were the only reason I breathed. And the only time I got on my knees was when I prayed please do not let him leave, please do not let him leave. You probably looked down on me and said my child, my child, what a fool, you want me to let you stay in this physical, this mental, this sexual abuse, I can't if I let you stay then to me you will be of no use. Why don't you come to me where the love is everlasting and true, where I can show you life after death, show you some things about me that you never knew. Show you your purpose and what you are really placed here to do. I want you to love me, I want you to worship me, glorify me and give all your praise to me. If you did it for them then why can't you do it for me why can't you be pleasing in my eyes.

Show me how to hold on

Show me how to hold on to a promise especially when it does not seem like its coming, there was once a time where I ran with the vision now I cannot keep from fumbling. You give me the words to keep me running, but I am moved by how I feel, my emotions and sight are going to get me in a whole lot of trouble. My vision was once clear but now it is blurred. I cannot tell the real from the fake I am seeing double. The word says A double minded mind cannot expect to receive nothing, I am a little shakey but still standing for something, no one is around so I invite you as my company because I need a better understanding of the things I am facing. Is this a fantasy or a dream I am chasing, you allowed the test to be placed right in my face. I am not weak by far, but these are some real life tribulations. There are times I want to quit but will not give in to temptation. I cut off some sidebar conversations because I want the truth..let us get to the bottom of these situations. The enemy brings so much deception and manipulation. I have been dealing with this for a long time. No need to do the calculation. Just want to be sure that I am not caught up in infatuation. Do not want to make false accusations, but this thing has me going through some pain, and if this is an assignment, then I am about to do some cancellation. I have sown where I want to go, if you have released my harvest, then I call forth manifestation. The enemy have brought some alternates and yes I have taken them into consideration, but I cannot have any hindrances trying to stop my elevation I am coming to you asking for a divine revelation. If this is not your path, then I am going to make a deviation. I cannot let this thing keep me bound. Because you have given me complete emancipation. This may seem like a one-sided conversation, but God has already spoken in Isaiah 55:11 when He said that His word does not return void. If God has given you a word, dream, or vision, hold on to it because it will surely come to pass.

You set me Free

You set me free I have been held captive for too long captive in my mind captive in wasted time, held captive in my wrong. Not doing your will but my own. It has been a while now and my true colors have really shown, you stripped me of everything old lovers, old friends everything gone. Even to the point where there is no family around just you and you alone. You put me in situations where there was no one call on no one to rely on. I do not regret it, in fact, I appreciate it. It brought me from my weakness and made me strong. I could not give you my all because of all the baggage I dragged along. Holding on to unforgiveness and bitterness it did not bring forth nourishment but rottenness to my bones. I find myself searching for answers that are already known. Because of too many voices in my ear like Gospel and secular music playing two different tones. But I thank God I know you for myself and in your word every promise made was a promise well kept. I am not one of the foolish virgins who missed the bridegroom because she slept. I know I gave a lot of me away but I offer you what I have left. There were many nights I slept after grieving the place where your holy spirit dwelt. Doing something foolish instead of telling you how I felt. I thank you for burning away my flesh like a candle when it melts. I stood on your word when I had nothing else. Could not be moved because my loins were girded with the belt. Now I am walking around with a pep in my step, remembering to reverance you with a continuous praise on my lips. I am going to drink from your well, and I am taking more than a sip. And I will not let you go until you bless me like Jacob with his limp. Like Jesus in the wilderness I won't be tempted, so I am going to keep my head bowed, knees kneeled down, no longer walking around with a frown, no longer mumbling my words but speaking them out loud, if I have made anyone I know I have made you proud, because I am no longer a hurt and wounded child, but a healed a whole woman now.

If you were mine

I see a King in you. A Leader and a Protector. A man of Authority and Power. An Overcomer an Anointed vessel. Someone, God has Chosen. A Royal Priesthood. If you were mine, I would help to "Cultivate" that; I would "Support" that, "Honor" that, "Respect" that. Not only will I Cater 2 u; I will minister to you. I'll do what other women are not willing to do. I will have the Devotion of Ruth I won't turn my back on you. I'll be your Esther. I'll fast 3 days and 3 nights no food or drink and even go before the King unsummoned for you.

#impatientlywaiting

About the Author

Shemeka McNair is a Mississippi native. She is a US Army Combat veteran that served in Operation Iraqi Freedom in the year of 2002. She was ordained a Minister in the year of 2009. She enjoys ministering and serving in all facets of ministry unto the Lord. She studied acting for film with New York Film Academy in Hollywood, California. She has been fortunate enough to write direct, and perform in her stage play production, "It's Well Worth the Wait." She looks forward to future endeavors in the area of theater arts and entertainment. She has served as a community activist with the organization Nuevo Sendero Inc. to help women who are victims and survivors of domestic violence and sexual assault. Also, serving with Jesus the Light of Light Outreach, Inc. which helps women and children in need, this Ministry focuses on meeting the needs of those who reach out locally in Central Florida area. She is the New Founder of the organization "Pink Diamonds & Black Onyx " Our Goal is to be a Support and a Resource to men in women in the area of Self-development, Relationships and Family.

www.ingramcontent.com/pod-product-compliance
Lightning Source LLC
Chambersburg PA
CBHW050724030426
42336CB00012B/1415